Power and Purpose

POWER AND PURPOSE

The Book of Revelation for Today

Russell L. Lackey

Afterword by Joel Patterson

RESOURCE *Publications* · Eugene, Oregon

Resource Publications
An Imprint of Wipf and Stock Publishers
199 W. 8th Ave., Suite 3
Eugene, OR 97401

www.wipfandstock.com

PAPERBACK ISBN: 978-1-4982-8916-0
HARDCOVER ISBN: 978-1-4982-8918-4
EBOOK ISBN: 978-1-4982-8917-7

Manufactured in the U.S.A.   08/12/16

For Jamie, Abigail, Sydney, Brenna, and Vicki

Contents

Introduction

THE BOOK OF REVELATION is confusing to read. Images of beasts, trumpets, plagues, and dragons fill its pages, intimidating the reader. Trying to navigate this ancient book requires great faith and imagination. Unfortunately, American Christianity lacks imagination.

I believe it is the church's lack of imagination that is pushing Millennials (those born between 1980 and 2000) away from church. In his book *You Lost Me*, David Kinnaman explains that Millennials are leaving the church at an alarming rate because they experience church to be overprotective, shallow, anti-science, simplistic toward sex, exclusive, and unwilling to provide room for doubt.[1] In other words, they are leaving because the church lacks the imagination to speak faithfully into their concerns.

How do we reverse this trend? How do we reengage the imagination of Millennials? Eugene Peterson suggests we pick up the book of Revelation. As Peterson explains: "I do not read the Revelation to get additional information about the life of faith in Christ, but to revive my imagination."[2]

As the campus pastor at Grand View University, a church-related school, I have watched students interact with the book of Revelation. These students have two things in common: first, they are very interested in Revelation; and second, they lack the tools to navigate this ancient book. I find this particularly disheartening

1. Kinnaman, *You Lost Me*, 92–93.
2. Peterson, *Reversed Thunder*, xi–xii.

because Revelation addresses many issues Millennials face: a distrust of economic and political structures, ecological concerns, complacency, and the difficulties of synthesizing faith with everyday life. Furthermore, Revelation assumes community, something Millennials value and are redefining in our culture.

The one consistent mistake I see students make when reading the book of Revelation is that they are asking the wrong question. They pick up Revelation trying to determine how the world will end. I understand this temptation. When things are difficult, people want to escape. However, this question causes people to read Revelation like a codebook that needs cracking. People in this camp jump from Daniel to 1 Thessalonians to Revelation with the hope of discovering a secret knowledge to make sure they will not be "left behind" when the rapture occurs.

But what if the question of Revelation isn't how will the world end, but rather, who is the Lord of this world?[3] Suddenly, everything changes. No longer can we read Revelation like a codebook. Rather, we have to read it as a whole, from start to finish, forcing us to discover how to serve the Lord even in the most difficult of situations. Christians who pick up Revelation with this question in mind do not try to escape society, rather, they work to reform it.

Reading Revelation as a whole shows that the book moves in a nonlinear way. Victorinus, writing in the third century, offers a helpful insight into Revelation's structure. Victorinus suggests we read Revelation like a spiral, with each loop consisting of a series of visions or cycles that teach us eternal truths about God, Jesus, the nature of evil, and ourselves. Expanding on Victorinus' insight, Craig Koester suggests: "Those who read Revelation as a whole encounter visions that alternatively threaten and assure them. With increasing intensity the vision at the bottom of the spiral threaten the readers' sense of security by confronting them. . . . Nevertheless, each time the clamor of conflict becomes unbearable, listeners are transported into the presence of God, the Lamb, and the heavenly chorus."[4]

---

3. Bauckham, *Theology of the Book of Revelation*, 8.

4. Koester, *Revelation and the End of All Things*, 39.

This book follows Victorinus' and Koester's lead as it is divided into six cycles: Life (Rev 1–3), Worthiness (Rev 4–7), Evangelism (Rev 8–11), Allegiance (Rev 12–15), Slavery (Rev 15–19), and Newness (Rev 19–22). Each cycle consists of two chapters with questions for further reflection. These questions are designed to aid a small group study or deepen individual reflection. However, do not let my questions be the only questions asked. Let your imaginations run wild as the truth of God's word intersects the realities of your life.

Finally, on a personal note, I would like to thank a few of the many people who made this book possible. First, I must thank Craig Koester for teaching me how to read the book of Revelation as well as my parents, Robert and Marie Lackey, for forming my imagination. Special thanks to Joel Patterson for his writing on this project and Aaron Snethen and Sarah Krumm for their design work. In addition, heartfelt gratitude to the staff at Wipf and Stock for their hard work and John and Cheryl Beran for their generous support. Finally, to my friends Kate Glenney, Mark Mattes, Ken Sundet Jones, Carol Henning and Alex Krumm, whose contributions and encouragement were so extensive that this book would not exist without them.

As you read this book, may your imaginations be stirred and your eyes opened to the Revelation of Jesus Christ. May you discover that true power and purpose comes from Christ, the Lamb who was slain.

Russell L. Lackey
Grand View University, Des Moines
St. Michael and All Angels Day 2016

CYCLE 1

LIFE

REVELATION 1

Jesus Is Alive

Fear not, I am the first and the last, and the living one. I died, and behold I am alive forevermore, and I have the keys of Death and Hades.

(Rev 1:17–18)

TWO THOUSAND YEARS AGO, a man named John found himself exiled and imprisoned on the island of Patmos off the coast of Asia Minor. His crime was finding life in God instead of wealth, military might, politics, or position. John saw the world through the lens of Jesus' resurrection. This powerful vision altered his life and compelled him to speak out no matter the cost. It made John a prophet.

Prophets are people who have seen God and are moved to speak. As the biblical scholar Abraham Heschel explains, "Prophets are some of the most disturbing people who have ever lived: the men whose inspiration brought the Bible into being—the men whose image is our refuge in distress, and whose voice and vision sustain our faith."[1] It is the prophet who has seen God and cries for "justice to roll down as waters."

The book of Revelation flows from a vision given to John by God. This vision offers an alternate way of seeing life. It calls us to pick a side. We must take a stand either with God or Satan, Good or Evil, Jesus or the Antichrist. Neutrality is not an option. Revelation is not an easy book to comprehend. Reading it might turn the whole world upside down. We might, however, gain a vision of what life truly is.

APOCALYPSE?

"Apocalypse" is the first word written in the book of Revelation. To understand this word, we need to face some misperceptions head on. Most hear the word and think of end-of-the-world scenarios such as global warming, terrorism, economic crashes, nuclear war, super viruses, race riots, meteorites, or even zombies.[2] But, in the Bible, "apocalypse" means something altogether different. Apocalypse simply means "to uncover." Think of the aroma that fills the kitchen as a pot of stew cooks on a stove. When it is time to eat, everyone gathers around the pot. When the lid is removed: "Apocalypse!"[3] That is what is happening in Revelation. God is cooking up a meal filled with good things. Our task is to lift the lid and dig in. Rather than fear, there is much promise in Revelation 1:1-3:

> The revelation of Jesus Christ, which God gave him to show to his servants the things that must soon take place. He made it known by sending his angel to his servant John, who bore witness to the word of God and to the testimony of Jesus Christ, even to all that he saw. Blessed is the one who reads aloud the words of this prophecy,

1. Heschel, *The Prophets*, ix.
2. Bendle, "Apocalyptic Imagination and Popular Culture," 1.
3. Peterson, *Reversed Thunder*, 19.

and blessed are those who hear, and who keep what is
written in it, for the time is near. (Rev 1:1–3)

It is understandable that many people think the book of Revelation is about the end of the world. In these first three verses we
hear about things that are "soon to take place" because the "time is
near." At first glance, this implies the end of the world. If we take a
closer look, however, we notice John does not say "the end" is near.
He simply says "the *time* is near." "Soon" and "near" are not meant
to signal the end of the world; rather, they clue us in to the immediacy of God. Like a mother who will soon deliver her child, the
time is near for God's salvation to occur. This is how God works.
"Know that the hour has come for you to wake from sleep. For
salvation is nearer to us now than when we first believed" (Rom
13:11). With God, it is always "soon" and "near" because salvation
is imminent.[4] It is with this sense of urgency that the rest of the
chapter unfolds.

SURPRISE: A LOVE LETTER

Most people would never associate Revelation with love. Instead,
they see it as God's judgment. Many preachers use Revelation to
threaten people to "turn or burn," that is, to choose heaven in order
to avoid hell. While there is judgment in Revelation, to focus solely
on that misses the point. At its heart, Revelation is a love letter.

> John to the seven churches that are in Asia: Grace to
> you and peace from him who is and who was and who
> is to come, and from the seven spirits who are before his
> throne, and from Jesus Christ the faithful witness, the
> firstborn of the dead, and the ruler of kings on earth. To
> him who loves us and has freed us from our sins by his
> blood and made us a kingdom, priests to his God and
> Father, to him be glory and dominion forever and ever.
> Amen. Behold, he is coming with the clouds, and every
> eye will see him, even those who pierced him, and all

4. Koester, *Revelation*, 222.

tribes of the earth will wail on account of him. Even so. Amen. "I am the Alpha and the Omega," says the Lord God, "who is and who was and who is to come, the Almighty." (Rev 1:4–8)

Like most letters in the ancient world, this one has a greeting that tells us about the sender. John is the author who is sent by Jesus, the faithful witness, the firstborn of the dead, and the ruler of the kings of earth. Each of Jesus' titles is important. Jesus is the "faithful witness." "Witness" in Greek is the same word for martyr. Jesus testified to God's love and was martyred on the cross. As the Apostle Paul tells us in the book of Romans, "But God shows his love for us in that while we were still sinners, Christ died for us" (Rom 5:8). Jesus' death is love in physical form.

We may ask whether Jesus' love is enough. Many people in history have sacrificed their lives for someone else. But Jesus' sacrifice is different. This is where his second title, "firstborn of the dead," makes all the difference. To be the "firstborn" means there will be others coming after him. Jesus died and rose again in order to raise us from the dead. His love is not only a life taken because of our sins; it is a resurrection for our eternity. Even more, Jesus' resurrection affirms his lordship over the "kings of the earth" who tried to contain him in the grave.

In the sixteenth century, church reformer Martin Luther initially saw Revelation as proof of God's wrath and condemnation. Before Luther's conversion, he hated God because he believed God punished sinners for not being holy enough. He rightly wondered why God would set an impossible standard that humans could never achieve. As Luther explains: "Though I lived as a monk without reproach, I felt that I was a sinner before God. I did not love, yes, I hated the righteous God who punishes sinners."[5] Until he truly came to know Jesus, all Luther thought God desired was perfect obedience. But then Luther discovered the love of God that sent Jesus to be our righteousness. This changed everything. It captured Luther. He said, "Here I felt that I was altogether born

5. Luther, *Career of the Reformer IV*, 336–37.

again and had entered paradise itself through open gates."[6] Luther was changed by the love of God that saves sinners. It is no accident that the opening words of Revelation mention this love because at its core, Revelation is a love letter.

THE WORD OF GOD

The word of God is powerful. After all, it was the word of God that created this world (Gen 1). It was the word of God that was placed into Jeremiah's mouth: "Behold, I have put my words in your mouth. See, I have set you this day over nations and over kingdoms, to pluck up and to break down, to destroy and to overthrow, to build and to plant" (Jer 1:9–10). With the word on his lips, Jeremiah had to proclaim the message of the Lord. In the same way, John has received the word and now must speak.

> I, John, your brother and partner in the tribulation and the kingdom and the patient endurance that are in Jesus, was on the island called Patmos on account of the word of God and the testimony of Jesus. I was in the Spirit on the Lord's day, and I heard behind me a loud voice like a trumpet saying, "Write what you see in a book and send it to the seven churches, to Ephesus and to Smyrna and to Pergamum and to Thyatira and to Sardis and to Philadelphia and to Laodicea." (Rev 1:9–11)

The word of God made John "a partner in the tribulation" (Rev 1:9) with other Christians and with Jesus himself. That is often what the word of God becomes for us because it is a living book. As the Epistle to the Hebrews says, "For the word of God is living and active, sharper than any two-edged sword, piercing to the division of soul and of spirit, of joints and of marrow, and discerning the thoughts and intentions of the heart" (Heb 4:12). The word of God put John where he was, exiled on the island of Patmos, but it also made him who he was.[7]

---

6. Ibid., 337.
7. Peterson, *Reversed Thunder*, 2.

> Then I turned to see the voice that was speaking to me,
> and on turning I saw seven golden lampstands, and
> in the midst of the lampstands one like a son of man,
> clothed with a long robe and with a golden sash around
> his chest. The hairs of his head were white, like white
> wool, like snow. His eyes were like a flame of fire, his feet
> were like burnished bronze, refined in a furnace, and his
> voice was like the roar of many waters. In his right hand
> he held seven stars, from his mouth came a sharp two-
> edged sword, and his face was like the sun shining in full
> strength. (Rev 1:12–16)

This vision is vastly different from the pictures of Jesus you see as a child. It is filled with images meant to hook the viewer. This picture (see fig. 1) is full of Old Testament imagery: the robe and golden sash are the uniform of the high priest (Exod 28:4), the white hair is the mark of the Ancient of Days (Dan 7:9), the bronze feet are a reminder of Ezekiel's angels (Ezek 1:7), and the voice of the roaring waters is the returning glory of God (Ezek 43:2).[8] Most striking, however, is the sword in Jesus' mouth. The sword, though not literally coming out of his mouth, symbolizes the powerful and dangerous two-edged truth of God's living word.

When I started my work as a pastor, I met a young man named Gabe who had read the book of Revelation and wanted to know why Jesus had laser-beam eyes (Rev 1:14). Gabe said, "I wish I had laser-beam eyes to melt my enemies." Gabe has been pained by many people in his life and, like most of us, believed revenge was the best option. I looked at Gabe and said, "You have something better than laser-beams, you have the word of God." He said, "I would rather have the eyes because the sword (word of God) means I have to tell people about Jesus instead of destroying them." Gabe got it. The word of God is alive and powerful.

8. Caird, *Revelation of Saint John*, 25.

St. John's Vision of Christ and the Seven Candlesticks
by Albrecht Dürer

III

Description (Figure 1): John is pictured kneeling before Jesus, who is in the center of the scene. The seven stars represent the seven angels and the seven lampstands represent the seven churches. It is important to note that the sword in Jesus' mouth is the only weapon Jesus uses. There is power in his word.

JESUS HOLDS THE KEYS

A friend of mine once told me about the cemetery where his sister-in-law was buried. Apparently, there was a road sign there that read: "One Way." Someday, all of us will travel this terrible road. Thankfully, however, Jesus has traveled down this path and offers a way out.

> When I saw him, I fell at his feet as though dead. But he laid his right hand on me, saying, "Fear not, I am the first and the last, and the living one. I died, and behold I am alive forevermore, and I have the keys of Death and Hades. Write therefore the things that you have seen, those that are and those that are to take place after this. As for the mystery of the seven stars that you saw in my right hand, and the seven golden lampstands, the seven stars are the angels of the seven churches, and the seven lampstands are the seven churches." (Rev 1:17–20)

What is the "revelation" of the book of Revelation? The answer is simple: Jesus is alive and has authority over death and hades. This might seem a bit underwhelming because of all the sensationalism surrounding the book of Revelation. Jesus' authority over death, however, is the most important statement ever made in human history. Biblical scholar Brian Blount explains, "Resurrection is God's silver bullet. When Jesus of Nazareth is raised from the depths of Hades, it is as though God, manipulating the dirt of the earth like the muzzle of a gun, shot him straight through the heart of an enemy. It is the resurrection that puts the enemy down."[9] Jesus has authority over death, it is the one inescapable reality that none of us can beat.

Think again about all the things that cause fear: global warming, terrorism, economic crashes, super viruses, race riots, meteorites, and those zombies. These and many other threats often paralyze us with fear because, like the pieces of a broken mirror, they reflect the painful reality that we will die. But Jesus holds the

---

9. Blount, *Invasion of the Dead*, 2.

keys to unlock death and hades. Once this truth takes hold, suddenly, everything is different. No longer is staying alive the challenge; rather, it is living as people who have *already overcome the grave.*

You can begin to see why John was exiled: people who believe that they will overcome death are dangerous. They do not need to bow their knees to the rulers of this age. They do not need to live lives paralyzed with fear. They have discovered that the very heart of God *is life. This* is the apocalypse, the uncovering: Jesus is alive! Oh, that we all would have such a vision of Jesus so that we, too, would live!

> *Be thou my vision, O Lord of my heart;*
> *Naught be all else to me, save that thou art;*
> *Thou my best thought, both by day or by night,*
> *Waking or sleeping, thy presence my light.*
>
> *Light of my soul, after victory won,*
> *May I reach heaven's joys, O heaven's Sun!*
> *Heart of my own heart, whatever befall,*
> *Still be my vision, O Ruler of all.*[10]

---

10. Irish Traditional, "Be Thou My Vision," *Evangelical Lutheran Worship* (Minneapolis: Augsburg Fortress, 2006), 793, verses 1, 4.

Refocus Questions

1. Before reading this chapter, what did you think the book of Revelation was about?

2. How does the Greek definition of *apocalypse* ("to uncover") change your perspective of Revelation?

3. John found himself exiled because of his faith in Jesus. Many preachers today say following Jesus will better your life. Which message do you believe? Why?

4. What description of Jesus is most striking to you?

5. If you knew that you could not die, what crazy thing would you do?

6. Why are Jesus' words to John so powerful (Rev 1:17–18)?

7. What are some questions you have about Revelation so far? (Let's see if they get answered throughout your study of Revelation).

REVELATION 2–3

What Will You Do with Your Life?

Let anyone who has an ear listen to what the Spirit is saying to the churches. To everyone who conquers, I will give permission to eat from the tree of life that is in the paradise of God. (Rev 2:7)

IN HER POEM "THE Summer Day," Mary Oliver asks the question: "Tell me, what is it you plan to do with your one wild and precious life?" This valuable question aims to encourage individuals to make life choices worthy of their unique lives. As a campus pastor I have watched too many students who are afraid to make any life decisions at all. These students want to lead exceptional lives, but they are afraid of making a mistake, choosing the wrong path, or missing a sign that will in turn ruin their chance of living their "one wild and precious life." It's a pity to see so many people paralyzed with fear.

But what if we are looking at this question from the wrong perspective? If we consider it from God's point of view, suddenly we are forced to ask different questions. Instead of wondering, "What I am supposed to do?" the question is, "Who has God created me to be?" Instead of wondering, "How do I attain a precious life?" the question is, "What precious thing is Christ calling me to give away?" Instead of wondering, "What choices must I make to live a wild life?" the question is, "What wild adventure is the Spirit leading me into?" It is true that we see though a glass dimly (1 Cor 13:12), but everything changes when our direction and our vision, like John's, comes from God and not ourselves.

Revelation 2 and 3 contain seven letters to the seven churches of Asia Minor (see fig. 2) that help us see our lives from God's point of view. The structure of each letter follows a basic pattern: (1) Address from Christ; (2) Words of rebuke and/or encouragement; and a (3) Promise to the conqueror.[1] In these two chapters, we get a glimpse of the life God wants for his church corporately and for his people individually. Some of these words are challenging and some are hard to hear. Christ is never afraid to confront his people. He does this in order to create a wild and precious live of faith for us to live.

Ephesus: God Wants You to Love

The first letter is addressed to the church at Ephesus which was one of the chief urban centers of the region. This coastal city on the eastern edge of what is now Turkey was a hub for commerce. The city had major streets and public squares, athletic festivals were held in its stadium, and its theater could hold up to twenty-four thousand people. Ephesus was also home to the temple of Artemis, one of the seven wonders of the ancient world.[2] To the Christians in this bustling city, Christ challenges them to love:

> To the angel of the church in Ephesus write: These are the words of him who holds the seven stars in his right hand, who walks among the seven golden lampstands: "I know your works, your toil and your patient endurance. I know that you cannot tolerate evildoers; you have tested those who claim to be apostles but are not, and

1. Koester, *Revelation and the End of All Things*, 56.
2. Ibid., 57–58.

The Seven Churches of Revelation

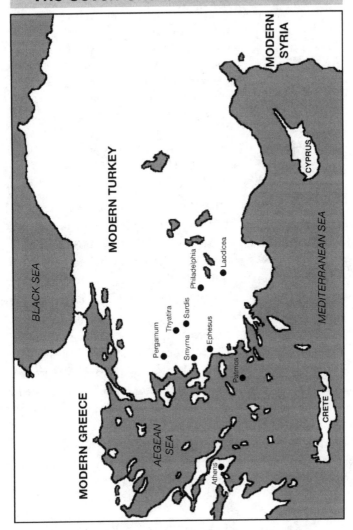

Description (Figure 2): When you compare the order of churches listed in Rev 2 and 3 to the map, you notice a pattern. The list of churches mentioned was the order in which mail would be delivered in Asia Minor. Mail would come to Ephesus and be distributed to Smyrna, Pergamum, Thyatira, Sardis, Philadelphia, and finally Laodicea.

have found them to be false. I also know that you are enduring patiently and bearing up for the sake of my name, and that you have not grown weary. But I have this against you, that you have abandoned the love you had at first. Remember then from what you have fallen; repent, and do the works you did at first. If not, I will come to you and remove your lampstand from its place, unless you repent. Yet this is to your credit: you hate the works of the Nicolaitans, which I also hate. Let anyone who has an ear listen to what the Spirit is saying to the churches. To everyone who conquers, I will give permission to eat from the tree of life that is in the paradise of God." (Rev 2:1–7)

In many respects, the church of Ephesus was the model church as they strove for truth and purity. However, in the midst of their striving, they forgot to love. This is disastrous because love is at the heart of God. It was out of love that God sent Jesus (John 3:16; Rom 5:8). As the Apostle Paul says, "If I give away all I have, and if I deliver up my body to be burned, but have not love, I gain nothing" (1 Cor 13:3).

Some people might object to this. They think love is too soft or trivial to be of serious importance. That cannot be further from the truth. Ask a soldier whose life was spared by the sacrifice of another soldier if love is soft. Or, ask my friend who forgave his wife after she had an affair. I have never witnessed such strength as when I watched him kneel alongside her at the communion rail, seeking the strength and forgiveness to hold their marriage together. Ephesus sought truth at the expense of love. A life without love is hardly the life God wants for us. Instead, God wants us to love.

Smyrna: God Wants You to Resist

For the residents of Smyrna life was comfortable because the city was so affluent. A harbor brought commerce to the region. The city streets were paved with stones and bordered by porticoes. Smyrna had a good library and a shrine to the famous Greek poet Homer. It was known for its beauty; for Christians, however, it was a place of suffering.[3] In this letter, Christ offers a word of hope to these persecuted people:

> And to the angel of the church in Smyrna write: These are the words of the first and the last, who was dead and came to life: "I know your affliction and your poverty, even though you are rich. I know the slander on the part of those who say that they are Jews and are not, but are a synagogue of Satan. Do not fear what you are about to suffer. Beware, the devil is about to throw some of you into prison so that you may be tested, and for ten days you will have affliction. Be faithful until death, and I will give you the crown of life. Let anyone who has an ear listen to what the Spirit is saying to the churches. Whoever conquers will not be harmed by the second death." (Rev 2:8–11)

Jesus is calling these persecuted Christians to "be faithful until death" (Rev 2:10). This is a bit unexpected. One would assume that Jesus would encourage them to wait for the persecution to end, but he doesn't. In our current culture, there is a terrible misconception that being a Christian is supposed to make life easy. Some preachers teach a message of prosperity that promises financial gain, healing, or some other miracle for the faithful. God does not promise this. In Matthew 16, Jesus tells his followers that they would have crosses to carry (Matt 16:24). The promise to persecuted Christians is never an easy life. The promise is that they will have real strength to endure.

What does this mean for us who are not persecuted? Elizabeth Schüssler Fiorenza suggests this passage calls us to "consistent resistance."[4] In other words, we are to resist the temptation of ease, the illusion of prosperity, and instead engage this world. Think of Samwise Gamgee in the *Lord of the Rings* trilogy, who said, "It's like in the great stories, the ones that really mattered. Full of darkness and danger they were, and sometimes you didn't want

---

3. Koester, *Revelation*, 271–82.
4. Schüssler Fiorenza, *Revelation*, 4.

to know the end because how could the end be happy? Those were the stories that stayed with you, that meant something even if you were too small to understand why. . . . In those stories folks had lots of chances of turning back, only they didn't. They kept going because they were holding onto something."[5] That is what Jesus promises. We can hold onto him. We might experience opposition, even persecution in this world, but we will find real strength to endure in the difficult present and the promise of eternal life in the future because Jesus holds the keys to death.

Pergamum: God Wants You to Be Different

The city of Pergamum came to prominence after the death of Alexander the Great. The last king of Pergamum, Attalus III, bequeathed his territory to Rome, which made the city the seat of government for the province. The city was built around a citadel hill that rose a thousand feet above the plains. On the summit was an acropolis with a massive altar to Zeus. In this letter, Christ speaks with the greatest authority in the very place political and religious power resided.[6]

> And to the angel of the church in Pergamum write: These are the words of him who has the sharp two-edged sword: "I know where you are living, where Satan's throne is. Yet you are holding fast to my name, and you did not deny your faith in me even in the days of Antipas my witness, my faithful one, who was killed among you, where Satan lives. But I have a few things against you: you have some there who hold to the teaching of Balaam, who taught Balak to put a stumbling block before the people of Israel, so that they would eat food sacrificed to idols and practice fornication. So you also have some who hold to the teaching of the Nicolaitans. Repent then. If not, I will come to you soon and make war against them with the

---

5. *The Lord of the Rings: The Return of the King*, directed by Peter Jackson, movie based on the novel by J. R. R. Tolkein (New Line Cinema, 2003).

6. Caird, *Revelation of Saint John*, 37.

sword of my mouth. Let anyone who has an ear listen
to what the Spirit is saying to the churches. To everyone
who conquers I will give some of the hidden manna, and
I will give a white stone, and on the white stone is written a new name that no one knows except the one who
receives it." (Rev 2:12–17)

The church at Pergamum is scolded for tolerating a teacher
named "Balaam" who instructed people to "eat food sacrificed to
idols and practice fornication" (Rev 2:14). The Old Testament false
prophet Balaam suggested that Israel be assimilated into the surrounding pagan culture in order to temper Israel's passion for God
(see Num 22–24). Assimilation was a problem for the Christians at
Pergamum. During religious festivals, the community gathered to
honor a god or goddess. An animal would be sacrificed and a banquet would follow. Everyone would attend this gathering. Festivals
would be held in the dining hall of a temple. What should a Christian do? What did this mean for Christians questioning whether
they should participate with their neighbors and non-Christian
friends? Should they go to preserve friendship? What if business
associates invite them? Should they go to maintain business? How
do they maintain their integrity? Assimilation was a real problem
for the early Christians.[7]

Times have not changed. Christians today face a similar
temptation to be like the surrounding culture. I have seen this
happen over and over again with high school and college students.
They love Jesus but are afraid of letting others know. Instead of
standing out, they hide in plain sight. I get it. I remember losing
friends when I became a Christian. This hurt a lot. But there is no
witness in being like everyone else. God has set apart Christians to
be witnesses (the word "sanctification" literally means "set apart").
The world needs Christians to be different. As Brennan Man-
ning explains, "The single greatest cause of atheism in the world
today is Christians, who acknowledge Jesus with their lips, then
walk out the door, and deny Him by their lifestyle. That is what

7. Collins, *Crisis and Catharsis*, 87–88.

an unbelieving world simply finds unbelievable." Fortunately for every friend I lost, I have gained many more who share with me a love of God.

To the church that fails to be different, Christ will come with his sword (that is, with God's Word) to challenge it (Rev 2:16). To the one who repents, they will be given a stone (which is like a ticket) of admittance to the heavenly banquet. God calls us to be different.

Thyatira: God Wants You to Know Truth

Thyatira was located in a broad valley southeast of Pergamum. As an important commercial center, Thyatira was home to many trade guilds. This included potters, tailors, leather workers, shoemakers, linen workers, bakers, coppersmiths, cloth dyers, and wool merchants. In the book of Acts we meet a merchant from Thyatira named Lydia who dealt in purple cloth (Acts 16:14).[8] In this letter, Christ calls a church known for love to seek truth.

> And to the angel of the church in Thyatira write: These are the words of the Son of God, who has eyes like a flame of fire, and whose feet are like burnished bronze: "I know your works—your love, faith, service, and patient endurance. I know that your last works are greater than the first. But I have this against you: you tolerate that woman Jezebel, who calls herself a prophet and is teaching and beguiling my servants to practice fornication and to eat food sacrificed to idols. I gave her time to repent, but she refuses to repent of her fornication. Beware, I am throwing her on a bed, and those who commit adultery with her I am throwing into great distress, unless they repent of her doings; and I will strike her children dead. And all the churches will know that I am the one who searches minds and hearts, and I will give to each of you as your works deserve. But to the rest of you in Thyatira, who do not hold this teaching, who have not learned what some

8. Koester, *Revelation and the End of All Things*, 61–62.

call 'the deep things of Satan,' to you I say, I do not lay on you any other burden; only hold fast to what you have until I come. To everyone who conquers and continues to do my works to the end, I will give authority over the nations; to rule them with an iron rod, as when clay pots are shattered—even as I also received authority from my Father. To the one who conquers I will also give the morning star. Let anyone who has an ear listen to what the Spirit is saying to the churches." (Rev 2:18–29)

The Christians at Thyatira were commended for their love (in contrast to the church at Ephesus). Nevertheless, they are rebuked for tolerating a false prophet who was teaching Christians to "practice fornication and to eat food sacrificed to idols" (Rev 2:20). The woman is nicknamed "Jezebel" to associate her with the infamous queen of Israel who promoted pagan worship (1 Kgs 18). Like Pergamum, the issue is assimilation.

Many might wonder why the Christians at Thyatira needed truth when they were known for love (Rev 2:19). Isn't love enough? In his book *Your Mind Matters*, John Stott explains, "Knowledge is indispensable to Christian life and service. If we do not use our mind which God has given us we condemn ourselves to spiritual superficiality." Stott goes on to say, "Knowledge leads us to higher worship, greater faith, deeper holiness, better service. What we need is not less knowledge but more knowledge."[9] Or as the Apostle Paul writes to the Corinthians: "Love does not rejoice in wrongdoing, but rejoices in the truth" (1 Cor 13:6). The mind matters. We love God and our neighbor with our heart, soul, strength, and mind (Luke 10:27–28). God wants you to know truth. There is no better way to know truth than to study God. As Charles Spurgeon explains, "The highest science, the loftiest speculation, the mightiest philosophy, which can ever engage the attention of a child of God, is the name, the nature, the person, the word, the doings, and the existence of the great God who that child calls Father."[10]

9. Stott, *Your Mind Matters*, 84.
10. Packer, *Knowing God*, 17.

Sardis: God Wants You to Speak Up

Sardis had a reputation for wealth because of gold found in a nearby river. Such wealth led to a community of abundance and tolerance. In fact, the Jewish community at Sardis was well-received and even had their own ritual-free food.[11] The Christians in the area were also very tolerant. They were the kind of people whom "everyone speaks well of, the perfect model of inoffensive Christianity."[12] Living in a diverse world, many believe tolerance to be a virtue. For Christians tolerance is a virtue as long as it does not lead to indifference. Christ wants us to engage others who are different, not ignore them. Listen to Jesus' words:

> And to the angel of the church in Sardis write: These are the words of him who has the seven spirits of God and the seven stars: "I know your works; you have a name of being alive, but you are dead. Wake up, and strengthen what remains and is on the point of death, for I have not found your works perfect in the sight of my God. Remember then what you received and heard; obey it, and repent. If you do not wake up, I will come like a thief, and you will not know at what hour I will come to you. Yet you have still a few persons in Sardis who have not soiled their clothes; they will walk with me, dressed in white, for they are worthy. If you conquer, you will be clothed like them in white robes, and I will not blot your name out of the book of life; I will confess your name before my Father and before his angels. Let anyone who has an ear listen to what the Spirit is saying to the churches." (Rev 3:1–6)

The Christians at Sardis were asleep (Rev 3:2). "Indifference" will do that. These Christians had tremendous resources to change the world but refused to use them because that would challenge the system. And why would they? When things are going well, it makes no sense to do anything that might cause persecution,

---

11. Hemer, *Letters to the Seven Churches*, 131.
12. Caird, *Revelation of Saint John*, 48.

imprisonment, exile, or death. During the time of Revelation, if people were exiled, their names would be blotted out of the city records. It is no surprise the Christians at Sardis played it safe.

Jesus, however, is not interested in the status quo. He loves the world too much to let it remain as it is. We Christians are called to speak up but, sadly, fail to do so. According to the Pew Research Center, "People are less likely to share their views in social media if they think their friends will disagree with them."[13] We need not be afraid to speak up. Christ's promise is that even if our names are "blotted out of the city records," if we get unfriended or unfollowed, our names will not be blotted out of the book of life. We will see later why this is so important. God wants us to speak up.

Philadelphia: God Wants You to Endure

The city of Philadelphia was situated in a rich, agricultural area whose volcanic soil was particularly suitable for vines. It had close ties to Rome and even adopted the family name of Emperor Flavius Vespasian (AD 69–79), calling itself Philadelphia Flavia. In contrast, the church in Philadelphia was small and poor. They were denounced by members of a local synagogue (Rev 3:9) and persecuted by Roman officials. However, what the members lacked in size and wealth, they made up with faith.[14] Listen to what Christ says to these poor Christians:

> And to the angel of the church in Philadelphia write: These are the words of the holy one, the true one, who has the key of David, who opens and no one will shut, who shuts and no one opens: "I know your works. Look, I have set before you an open door, which no one is able to shut. I know that you have but little power, and yet you have kept my word and have not denied my name. I will make those of the synagogue of Satan who say that they are Jews and are not, but are lying—I will make them

13. Hampton et al., "Social Media and the 'Spiral of Silence.'"
14. Hemer, *Letters to the Seven Churches*, 153–58.

come and bow down before your feet, and they will learn that I have loved you. Because you have kept my word of patient endurance, I will keep you from the hour of trial that is coming on the whole world to test the inhabitants of the earth. I am coming soon; hold fast to what you have, so that no one may seize your crown. If you conquer, I will make you a pillar in the temple of my God; you will never go out of it. I will write on you the name of my God, and the name of the city of my God, the new Jerusalem that comes down from my God out of heaven, and my own new name. Let anyone who has an ear listen to what the Spirit is saying to the churches." (Rev 3:7–13)

The Christian life often leads to rejection. Jesus was rejected. His followers are often rejected. Jesus said, "Daughters of Jerusalem, do not weep for me, but weep for yourselves and for your children . . . for if they do these things when the wood is green, what will happen when it is dry?" (Luke 23:28–31). In other words, if people persecuted Christ, then his followers should expect to be persecuted as well.

A temptation that arises from the threat of persecution is to simply escape it. This desire has manifested itself in the way some Christians have used Revelation 3:10 as a proof text for a new view of the "rapture." Historically, the rapture was understood to occur when Christ returns at his second coming and "calls up" Christians to join him. This view changed in the early 1800s when a man named John Nelson Darby suggested that Christ would "call up" Christians into heaven in order to spare them from a global persecution known as the "hour of trial" (Rev 3:10). According to this view, Christ's second coming will occur between three and seven years after the rapture has occurred. The *Left Behind* series popularized this new understanding of the rapture. For those who hold this view, the hope for Christians is to escape persecution.

Another temptation that arises from the threat of persecution is to simply give up one's convictions and join their persecutors. This is understandable. It is hard to stand out. It is hard to maintain faith when people feel alone. It is hard to believe Christians "conquer eternally" when their earthly existence is filled with strife.

In college, I decided to become a pastor. My girlfriend at the time told me she would never be a pastor's wife. This crushed me because I loved her. We broke up over it. For the next couple years, I was rejected many times by women who did not want to be married to a pastor. There were many times that I wondered if it was worth it. When I met the woman who became my wife, I found it was worth holding onto my convictions.

Jesus promises to give strength to those who are persecuted. The hope is not escape; it is endurance. Jesus is with his church and will keep it. He will give them a crown and make them pillars in the temple of God (Rev 3:12). In other words, we who endure have a place near God. Society may view us as outsiders, but Christ makes us insiders in his realm. God wants us to endure.

Laodicea: God Wants You to Have Passion

Christ introduces himself to the church of Laodicea as the true witness. This is ironic because the church does not seem to know the truth about itself. The Laodicean citizen would say, "I am rich . . . and need nothing" (Rev 3:17). In fact, after an earthquake in AD 60, the Laodiceans refused gold from Rome to rebuild their city. The truth is that even though they thought they were rich, Christ called these Christians poor.[15] Listen to Christ's words:

> And to the angel of the church in Laodicea write: The words of the Amen, the faithful and true witness, the origin of God's creation: "I know your works; you are neither cold nor hot. I wish that you were either cold or hot. So, because you are lukewarm, and neither cold nor hot, I am about to spit you out of my mouth. For you say, 'I am rich, I have prospered, and I need nothing.' You do not realize that you are wretched, pitiable, poor, blind, and naked. Therefore I counsel you to buy from me gold refined by fire so that you may be rich; and white robes to clothe you and to keep the shame of your nakedness

---

15. Hemer, *Letters to the Seven Churches*, 186–91.

from being seen; and salve to anoint your eyes so that you may see. I reprove and discipline those whom I love. Be earnest, therefore, and repent. Listen! I am standing at the door, knocking; if you hear my voice and open the door, I will come in to you and eat with you, and you with me. To the one who conquers I will give a place with me on my throne, just as I myself conquered and sat down with my Father on his throne. Let anyone who has an ear listen to what the Spirit is saying to the churches." (Rev 3:14–22)

Outside of Laodicea there was a natural hot spring as well as a mountain spring whose fresh water ran cold. There was also a Roman aqueduct that brought water into the city. The aqueduct was lukewarm and smelled awful. No one would drink this putrid water unless it was absolutely necessary. In calling these Christians "lukewarm," Jesus likens them to this putrid water. They think they have everything, but Christ says they are as wretched, pitiable, poor, blind, and naked as the putrid, lukewarm water of the aqueduct.

Many of us can see ourselves in this metaphor. The world has convinced us that life is found in social media, craft beer, material possessions, stylish beards, and the like. There is nothing wrong with such things unless we believe life is found in such things. When that happens, these good things become "putrid" things. God wants us to drink the living water that flows from his throne. This water is both hot and cold. This water leads to passionate living instead of a lukewarm existence. God wants us to have passion.

What should each of us plan to do with our "one wild and precious life?" The answer is simple: God wants us to love, resist, be different, know truth, speak up, endure, and have passion. In other words, he wants us to be free and fully engaged. Remember, the revelation of Revelation is that Jesus is alive. Jesus wants us to live. We do not have to be paralyzed thinking that one bad choice will ruin our entire life. Follow Jesus. He who holds the keys to death and hades will lead you on a wild adventure.

Refocus Questions

1. Do you know anyone like Ephesus (always right but not always loving)? Why do you think love is so important to God?

2. To Smyrna and Philadelphia, Christ promises that they would continue to suffer. How does this admonition challenge your faith? Also, Jesus promises to be with them in their suffering. How does this encourage your faith?

3. Pergamum and Thyatira struggled with assimilation. Why should Christians be different from the world in which they live? Why it is so hard to do this?

4. If Ephesus struggled with love, Thyatira struggled with truth. Why is truth so important for Christians? Why do our minds matter? How can love and truth work together?

5. Sardis was a wealthy church that was unwilling to speak out about the "wrongs" all around them. Why do you think Christ threatened to come to them as a thief? What might Jesus want to steal from them? What are some things Christ might have to take from you?

6. Why is God so disgusted with "lukewarm Christianity?" What are some areas in your faith that you consider are "lukewarm?"

7. Looking at these seven churches, to which do you most closely relate? Why? How are you challenged by this?.

CYCLE 2

WORTHINESS

REVELATION 4–5

Jesus Is Worthy

And I began to weep bitterly because no one was found worthy to open
the scroll of to look into it. (Rev 5:4)

IF YOU LOOK CLOSELY, you might spot a shift in the business world.
It might not seem dramatic, but it is. Profits are no longer the sole
metric for measuring a corporation's value. Instead, customers
are taking corporate behavior into consideration when they make
their purchases. Consumers want a company with ethics, not just
sales. Economist Laurie Bassi explains, "More and more, compa-
nies must be good to succeed. That is, they have to be good to their
customers, good to their employees, as well as good stewards of the
communities they touch."[1] In the new social marketplace, worthiness counts! Think about Walmart. This retailer offers low prices
to consumers; however, it is also accused of paying employees low
wages. As a result, many have deemed Walmart an "unworthy"
company. In the long run, that could spell significant loss in profits
for Walmart and dissatisfaction from its shareholders.

1. Bassi, *Good Company*, 4.

There is nothing new in determining a thing's value; we even do this with people. A sports star is worthy of a large contract because she wins matches or he scores touchdowns. Actors are worthy of multimillion dollar contracts because their name above the title on a movie poster assures box office sales. In these cases, value is based upon the ability to monetize unique gifts. What would happen if the *standard* changed and we measured worth by the positive impact an individual had on society? Suddenly teachers would make more money and athletes much less.

Is it possible for God to be judged in the same way? Can we measure God's worthiness? If so, what standard do we use? More to the point: what makes Jesus worthy? The answers to these questions are important not because of what they reveal about God, but because of what they reveal about us and why we worship God and Jesus. Thankfully, these very questions are answered in Revelation 4 and 5.

GOD IS WORTHY OF WORSHIP

Revelation 4 begins with John being *called into the heavenly throne room* (see fig. 3). John is not the first human to be summoned to the divine throne room. When they were called, the prophets Isaiah, Daniel, and Ezekiel all stood before God in the throne room. In fact, when Isaiah saw God, he said, "Woe is me! For I am lost; for I am a man of unclean lips, and I dwell in the midst of a people of unclean lips; for my eyes have seen the King, the Lord of hosts!" (Isa 6:5). Isaiah was overwhelmed by the holiness of God. John's vision is no different. His senses are overwhelmed by colors, sounds, and movements that fill the chamber. In the center of the room is God who is surrounded by elders wearing golden crowns and creatures flying through the air while praising God.

> After this I looked, and behold, a door standing open in heaven! And the first voice, which I had heard speaking to me like a trumpet, said, "Come up here, and I will show you what must take place after this." At once I was in the Spirit, and behold, a throne stood in heaven,

St. John with the Twenty-Four Elders
by Albrecht Dürer

IV

Description (Figure 3): John is pictured in the center of the scene. Below him is earth. Above John is the heavenly throne room into which he is called (Rev 4). God is on the throne surrounded by the heavenly hosts. On God's lap is a scroll. Next to him is the lamb who alone is worthy to open the scroll.

with one seated on the throne. And he who sat there had the appearance of jasper and carnelian, and around the throne was a rainbow that had the appearance of an emerald. Around the throne were twenty-four thrones, and seated on the thrones were twenty-four elders, clothed in white garments, with golden crowns on their heads. From the throne came flashes of lightning, and rumblings and peals of thunder, and before the throne were burning seven torches of fire, which are the seven spirits of God, and before the throne there was as it were a sea of glass, like crystal. And around the throne, on each side of the throne, are four living creatures, full of eyes in front and behind: the first living creature like a lion, the second living creature like an ox, the third living creature with the face of a man, and the fourth living creature like an eagle in flight. And the four living creatures, each of them with six wings, are full of eyes all around and within, and day and night they never cease to say, "Holy, holy, holy, is the Lord God Almighty, who was and is and is to come!" (Rev 4:1–8)

Before we look at God, let us first consider the twenty-four elders and four creatures. Some have said the elders are the twelve sons of Jacob along with the twelve apostles. It is more likely they are a picture of the martyrs we learned about earlier who are promised white robes (Rev 3:5), crowns (Rev 2:10), and a place on Christ's throne (Rev 3:21). The four creatures represent all of creation as their faces resemble a lion, an ox, a human, and an eagle.[2] These four creatures symbolize what is noblest, strongest, wisest and swiftest in all creation. The fact that they have a multitude of eyes "all around and within" means they are connected to everything in creation and are able to see the core of every single thing that exists. No wonder Isaiah said, "Woe is me."

What is most important about these heavenly citizens is not who they are but what they do. The elders, whom we and John might at first regard as deserving of admiration, deflect attention. They know that God alone is worthy of worship and thus cast

2. Koester, *Revelation*, 369.

down their golden crowns in a gesture of humility and deference to God's worthiness. The creatures who *see all* add their voices in praising God.

> And whenever the living creatures give glory and honor and thanks to him who is seated on the throne, who lives forever and ever, the twenty-four elders fall down before him who is seated on the throne and worship him who lives forever and ever. They cast their crowns before the throne, saying, "Worthy are you, our Lord and God, to receive glory and honor and power, for you created all things, and by your will they existed and were created."
> (Rev 4:9–11)

Everything about this vision points to why God is worshiped. God is in the center of the room because God is the center of all reality. God is also called the creator of all things (Rev 4:11). Without God, we would cease to exist. Reflecting on this truth, the Apostle Paul said, "In God we live and move and have our being" (Acts 17:28). We can say we worship God because we were made to worship God. Saint Augustine of Hippo wrote: "You *have made us for yourself, O Lord, and our heart is restless until it rests in you.*"[3]

There is more. God does not simply make us and leave us alone like a clockmaker winds the springs and leaves a clock to run. No, God continues to care for us and this world. The rainbow around the throne is an allusion to the covenant God made with Noah.[4] In the book of Genesis, God delivered Noah and his family through the chaos and destruction of the flood. When the water receded, God provided a rainbow as a sign that he would never food the earth again (Gen 9:8–17). The sign of the rainbow reminds us of God's ongoing care and tells us that God deserves worship.

With all of this talk about the kindness of God, we must not forget that God is holy! C. S. Lewis highlights this in his book, *The Lion, the Witch, and the Wardrobe.* There is a powerful scene

---

3. Augustine, *Confessions*, 1:1.
4. Caird, *Revelation of Saint John*, 63.

in which the girl Susan, who has come as a stranger to Narnia, learns about the lion Aslan, who is the creator of Narnia. In the story, Mr. Beaver tells Susan that "Aslan is a lion, the great Lion." Susan responds by saying, "Ooh, I thought he was a man. Is he quite safe? I shall feel rather nervous about meeting a lion." Mr. Beaver responds, "Safe? Who said anything about safe? Of course he isn't safe. But he's good. He's the King, I tell you."[5]

God is the creator of all things. God is powerful. God is not safe but God is good. God takes care of us. He is our maker and our keeper. As the psalmist says, "The Lord will keep you from all evil; he will keep your life. The Lord will keep your going out and your coming in from this time forth and forevermore" (Ps 121:7–8). The Lord is the eternal God seated on the throne.

It's typical and tragic for sinners like us to worship other things instead of God. Think about the millions of people who gather on Sundays in homes and in corporate-sponsored stadiums to cheer on their favorite football team instead of attending church. They are loyal to a team that might win or might lose, a team that does not know anything about them. Or we worship popularity, status, financial security, or individual freedom. Whatever the object of our worship, none of them can give what they promise. God, on the other hand, made us. God knows everything about us. God is the creator who speaks and reveals, creates and redeems, orders and blesses.[6] God is faithful to his creation and worthy of all praise. This is why we worship. This is why the elders cast down their golden crowns. This is why the four creatures sing.[7]

When we worship like the elders and creatures, we discover the beauty of worship. In praising God, we begin to understand the psalmist's words: "O taste and see that the Lord is good" (Ps 34:8). It's like eating a special meal with food that makes the saliva flow; when we can't eat another bite, we still wish we could keep tasting and delighting in it. Our worship causes us to hunger and crave

---

5. Lewis, *The Lion, the Witch, and the Wardrobe*, 77–81.

6. Peterson, *Reversed Thunder*, 59.

7. Bauckham, *Theology of the Book of Revelation*, 51–53.

more of God because we were made by God and nothing else will satisfy us.

CREATURES ARE UNWORTHY

Revelation 5 shifts our focus from God to the scroll on his lap. Some students of the Bible think the scroll is the book of life mentioned throughout Revelation (Rev 3:5; 13:8; 17:8; 20:12; 21:27). Others suggest that the scroll is God's redemptive history, the actual scroll Jesus read from in the synagogue (Luke 4:21), or the revelation about the end of the world. Even though there is much speculation about what the scroll contains, Revelation cares about something that's way more important; the main point in this passage is that *no one is worthy* to open the scroll.

> Then I saw in the right hand of him who was seated on the throne a scroll written within and on the back, sealed with seven seals. And I saw a mighty angel proclaiming with a loud voice, "Who is worthy to open the scroll and break its seals?" And no one in heaven or on earth or under the earth was able to open the scroll or to look into it, and I began to weep loudly because no one was found worthy to open the scroll or to look into it. (Rev 5:1–4)

In the midst of such splendor and vitality, John becomes painfully and personally aware that no one is worthy to open the scroll.[8] Surely someone should be able to open it. There have been amazing people who have lived: Whether it's the Buddha or Mohammed, Martin Luther or Martin Luther King, Gandhi or Mother Theresa, a first grade teacher or a personal hero, none of them are worthy to open the scroll. Even if someone's life has influenced billions of people, they're not worthy. No one is.

At first glance, this might appear to be a judgment against other religions. It isn't. Rather, it is a judgment against humanity. Even though humanity has been "crowned with glory" (Ps 8:5), we

---

8. Peterson, *Reversed Thunder*, 64.

are still part of creation and thus unworthy to open the scroll. Help must come from outside of creation. Help must come from God.

> And one of the elders said to me, "Weep no more; behold, the Lion of the tribe of Judah, the Root of David, has conquered, so that he can open the scroll and its seven seals." And between the throne and the four living creatures and among the elders I saw a Lamb standing, as though it had been slain, with seven horns and with seven eyes, which are the seven spirits of God sent out into all the earth. (Rev 5:5–6)

John's tears are interrupted by a declaration: A *champion* has been found who is worthy to open the scroll. The champion is the Lion from the tribe of Judah, the descendant of David. In the Old Testament, King David was regarded as a mighty warrior who fought like a lion and conquered his enemies. Israel had waited for a descendant of David to be their champion (Isa 11).

When John looks for the lion, what he actually sees is a lamb who was slaughtered and yet lives. This is significant. As Craig Koester explains, "What John hears about the Lion recalls promises from the Old Testament, and what he sees in the Lamb reflects the crucifixion of Christ."[9] The Lion fulfills the prophet's declaration to Israel that God would send them a powerful ruler. The slain lamb is also a powerful reminder that Jesus' mercy and salvation comes to us on the cross and that only he can triumph over death itself. One might expect the Lion to be the stronger of the two images, but the slain lamb is much stronger. As Brian Blount rightly explains, "For God to save us, God must invade. God's primary weapon is resurrection, the Lamb's resurrection."[10] It is the crucified, died, and resurrected Jesus who is worthy to open the scroll.

In college, I had a coach who disliked Christianity because he saw the cross as a sign of weakness. This idea is not new. The early church father Justin Martyr said, "They [critics of Christianity] say that our madness consists in the fact that we put a crucified man in

---

9. Koester, *Revelation and the End of All Things*, 78.
10. Blount, *Invasion of the Dead*, 21.

second place after the unchangeable and eternal God, the Creator of the world."[11] Fighting a similar criticism, the Apostle Paul wrote:

> For since, in the wisdom of God, the world did not know God through wisdom, it pleased God through the folly of what we preach to save those who believe. For Jews demand signs and Greeks seek wisdom, but we preach Christ crucified, a stumbling block to Jews and folly to Gentiles, but to those who are called, both Jews and Greeks, Christ the power of God and the wisdom of God. (1 Cor 1:21–24)

The cross looks like weakness but it is actually God's strength. Jesus is the Lion of Judah. He uses his power to conquer the grave and give us life. Jesus is the Lamb who dies in order to conquer the grave. It is this sacrifice that makes him worthy to open the scroll. It is this sacrifice that makes him worthy of our worship.

John's experience of these events moves him to tears. John cried because no one was worthy to open the scroll. We can understand this. All of us have been disappointed in people, in life, in circumstances, and in ourselves. Such disappointment often leads to tears. It is okay to cry. What's not okay is to believe that, since we are unworthy, we should do nothing to fix our world. We must not fall into this trap. Instead, we should allow our tears to inspire us to action. This is what Christians have done throughout history. Many of the hospitals in our communities were founded by Christian denominations: Lutheran, Methodist, Presbyterian, and Catholic. It is Christians who weep over society's brokenness who find the motivation for sacrificial action. We are not worthy because we build hospitals; however, our tears lead us to do worthy things.

---

11. Hengel, *Crucifixion*, 1.

WORTHY IS THE LAMB

Jesus is worshiped in the remaining verses of ch. 5. Not only do the elders and four creatures worship Jesus, but the scene enlarges to include every living creature on and under the earth.

> And he went and took the scroll from the right hand of him who was seated on the throne. And when he had taken the scroll, the four living creatures and the twenty-four elders fell down before the Lamb, each holding a harp, and golden bowls full of incense, which are the prayers of the saints. And they sang a new song, saying, "Worthy are you to take the scroll and to open its seals, for you were slain, and by your blood you ransomed people for God from every tribe and language and people and nation, and you have made them a kingdom and priests to our God, and they shall reign on the earth."
>
> Then I looked, and I heard around the throne and the living creatures and the elders the voice of many angels, numbering myriads of myriads and thousands of thousands, saying with a loud voice, "Worthy is the Lamb who was slain, to receive power and wealth and wisdom and might and honor and glory and blessing!" And I heard every creature in heaven and on earth and under the earth and in the sea, and all that is in them, saying, "To him who sits on the throne and to the Lamb be blessing and honor and glory and might forever and ever!" And the four living creatures said, "Amen!" and the elders fell down and worshiped. (Rev 5:7–14)

God is worshiped for being the creator. Jesus is worshiped because he overcomes death. This is the heart of worship. Notice the heart is not a style of worship. There is no mention of hymnals, denominations, liturgy, projection screens, organs, bands, or worship space. Instead, worship occurs when we join the rest of creation in faithful praise of God and the Lamb. We cannot stand back as spectators. Either the promise of the Lamb draws all of who we are and causes us to sing, or we will reject him and remain silent. Either we acknowledge Jesus as worthy or we will fail to do so. The four living creatures affirm the good news of the Lamb's sacrificed life when they say, "Amen!" (Rev 5:14). Amen means "yes" or "agreed." God and the Lamb are worthy of all praise.

Worthy is the Lamb who was slain
Holy, holy is He
Sing a new song to Him who sits on
Heaven's mercy seat

Holy, holy, holy is the Lord God Almighty
Who was and is and is to come
With all creation I sing praise to the King of kings
You are my everything and I will adore You.[12]

12. Jennie L. Riddle, "Revelation Song" (Gateway Create, 2004), chorus.

Refocus Questions

1. Today, star athletes, actors, and CEOs are paid tremendous amounts of money for being "worthy." As stated above, often it is levels of success that determine worthiness. How does Jesus redefine how worthiness is measured?

2. To quote C. S. Lewis: "The ancient person approached God (or even the gods) as the accused person approached a judge. For the modern man, the roles are reversed. We are the ones who judge and God is the one on trial."[13] In what ways do you put God on trial?

3. How important is it that no one was found worthy to open the scroll except Jesus? Does this mean Jesus narrows the focus of worship (i.e., he is the only one to worship) or does this actually expand our worship (i.e., without Jesus there would be no one to worship)?

4. Do you think Revelation 5 hinders a Christian's relationship with people of other religions? How might Revelation 5 open Christians up to other religions?

5. How do you see Jesus: as the Lion or the Lamb? How is it helpful to see Jesus as both the Lion *and* the Lamb?

6. In these chapters, there is a contrast between God's power on the throne and Christ's power demonstrated in weakness. How do these contradictory images hold together? What power does weakness hold?

7. Jesus' sacrifice is the inspiration for worship. In your experience, where do you see the death and resurrection of Jesus as the inspiration for a church's worship? Is the message primarily about Jesus or is the focus on something else?

13. Lewis, *God in the Dock*, 244.

REVELATION 6–7

Are You Worthy?

For the great day of their wrath has come, and who can stand?
(Rev 6:17)

WHERE WERE YOU ON 9/11? Perhaps you weren't even born yet. I had just graduated from seminary. My wife was in her second year teaching elementary school. When she heard of the attack, her legs gave way and she had to sit down. However, she could not remain sitting. She had a classroom filled with fifth graders who needed her to maintain a non-anxious, peaceful environment in the midst of turmoil. Where would she find the strength? Collecting herself, she silently prayed, asking Jesus for strength. Then, she rose and led her class.

Life is often like this. One moment everything is fine. The next moment, a medical test, car accident, job loss, or mass shooting turns everything upside down. At such times, our instinct is to try to regain control; but, some things just cannot be controlled. Jesus tells a parable about a man who tries to control his destiny only to have his life taken from him the very night his plan was in place (Luke 12:13–24). So, what are we to do when towers crumble? Where do we find strength in the midst of weakness? How do we stand when our legs give way?

EXPOSING FALSE SECURITY

Revelation 6 begins with the Lamb, who is the only one found worthy, opening the scroll. As the Lamb unlocks each of the seven seals of the scroll, John is invited by the living creatures to "come" near. What he sees are four riders who usher in violence and warfare.

> Now I watched *when the Lamb opened one of the seven seals*, and I heard one of the four living creatures say with a voice like thunder, "Come!" And I looked, and behold, a white horse! And its rider had a bow, and a crown was given to him, and he came out conquering, and to conquer.
>
> *When he opened the second seal*, I heard the second living creature say, "Come!" And out came another horse, bright red. Its rider was permitted to take peace from the earth, so that people should slay one another, and he was given a great sword.
>
> *When he opened the third seal*, I heard the third living creature say, "Come!" And I looked, and behold, a black horse! And its rider had a pair of scales in his hand. And I heard what seemed to be a voice in the midst of the four living creatures, saying, "A quart of wheat for a denarius, and three quarts of barley for a denarius, and do not harm the oil and wine!"
>
> *When he opened the fourth seal*, I heard the voice of the fourth living creature say, "Come!" And I looked, and behold, a pale horse! And its rider's name was Death, and Hades followed him. And they were given authority over a fourth of the earth, to kill with sword and with famine and with pestilence and by wild beasts of the earth. (Rev 6:1–8, italics mine)

Commonly called the "Four Horsemen of the Apocalypse," these frightening riders have long captured our imagination. An online search will reveal a cadre of references in movies, art, books, sporting events, and music. Usually, references to the Four Horsemen are used for intimidation. However, in Revelation they reveal God's righteous cause. In his woodcut, the Reformation-era artist Albrecht Dürer does a masterful job depicting the scene (see fig. 4). The purpose of the riders' entry is to expose the many things we trust for security other than God: nation, civil peace, wealth, and health. The four riders expose the shortcomings of such misguided trust.

In Nation We Trust—the first rider (Rev 6:1–2) is armed with a bow. The most famous bowmen of John's time came from Parthia, the region that lay beyond the Roman Empire's eastern frontier. The Parthian forces featured mounted archers and drove back the Roman army in 53 BC, 36 BC, and AD 62. The great Roman Empire could not conquer the Parthians. As Craig Koester notes, "The Parthians were a nagging reminder about the limits of the security that Rome could provide."[1] Kingdoms end. Governments fall apart. *Do not place your trust in the nation!*

In Peace We Trust—the second rider (Rev 6:3–4) wields a great sword and "was permitted to take peace from the earth." The sword was a symbol of the *Pax Romana* (Roman Peace). Rome believed a sword was necessary to pacify communities. But is pacification the same as peace? The second rider challenges the idea of peacekeeping by any human means or might. *Do not place your trust in peace at all costs.*

In Wealth We Trust—the third rider (Rev 6:5–6) holds a pair of scales like those used in the commerce of the ancient marketplace. The threat is of economic hardship where wheat and barley are purchased at extremely high prices whereas luxury items (oil and wine) can be purchased at normal prices. In this scenario, "the wealthy continue to live as usual but the crisis hurts the poor."[2] This is a case of economic injustice. Thankfully, Revelation addresses this later in ch. 18. *Do not place your trust in wealth.*

---

1. Koester, *Revelation and the End of All Things*, 84.
2. Boring, *Revelation*, 122.

The Four Horsemen by Albrecht Dürer

V

Description (Figure 4): The four riders of the apocalypse are pictured here. Notice how Dürer positions the horses so that the starving horse of death (bottom left-hand corner) is nearest to the viewer.

In Health We Trust—the fourth rider (Rev 6:7–8) rides a sickly, green horse followed by death. If famine specifically harmed the poor, disease affects all social classes. None will escape. Death follows the destruction the previous riders bring. *Do not place your trust in health.*

How do we make sense of the vision of these four riders? It is easy to understand why we should not trust such things. However, how can we trust a God who allows such devastation to occur? This question is not easily answered and Revelation does not attempt to do so. Instead, it recognized that forces exist in the world and they bring about evil. God is not the author of evil, but evil still exists.

There is another way to look at this vision. We get a clue from the African American spiritual "Wade in the Water," which speaks of God "troubling the water." The image implies God shaking things up in order to accomplish his purposes. In his "Letter from the Birmingham Jail," Martin Luther King Jr., challenged local clergy and the nation itself to rise to action. As Edward Gilbreath explains, "In Birmingham, King was able to both write and practice a holistic vision of what it means to be a Christian in a broken and unjust world in order to inspire both individuals and communities to reexamine their relationship to justice."[3] King's willingness to trouble the water exposed the hypocrisy and injustice of segregation. In the same way, the four riders trouble the earth in order to expose the evil and idolatry that subject people to death.

With a bit of logic, we can understand how this works. Before 9/11, most Americans felt secure from foreign threats. At the very least, their own soil was secure. That false security crumbled when the terrorists steered a plane into the first tower. Many think America is a land of peace, but police brutality occurs and communities explode. The "Black Lives Matter" movement has shown the futility in blind allegiance to civil authority. Many believe in the almighty dollar only to have the Great Recession expose the holes in the economic system. If we survive all of these plagues, we

3. Gilbreath, *Birmingham Revolution*, 167–69.

know that viruses such as ebola, swine flu, SARS, and zika traverse the planet, killing indiscriminately. The four riders aren't simply scary adversaries; they have a righteous cause.

We must, of course, ask if God could be the cause of these things. This question is not easily answered. Clearly, human sin, evil, and God's sovereignty must be considered when asking this question. It is clear that God is present even when we are surrounded by trouble and turmoil. Somehow, God is there working for the good. As the book of Romans says, "We know that all things work together for good for those who love God, who are called according to his purpose" (Rom 8:28). We do not know exactly how God is working. Paul says in 1 Corinthians 13, that we see through a glass dimly. But we do know that in love, God is willing to trouble the water.

> *Wade in the water*
> *Wade in the water, children*
> *Wade in the water*
> *God's gonna trouble the water.*[4]

THE MARTYRS TAKE A MUCH NEEDED REST

It would be great to say things get better in the second half of ch. 6, but they don't. The unlocking of the next two seals further unsettles notions of safety as the martyrs rest in heaven even as the inhabitants of the earth experience the Lamb's wrath.

> *When he opened the fifth seal,* I saw under the altar the souls of those who had been slain for the word of God and for the witness they had borne. They cried out with a loud voice, "O Sovereign Lord, holy and true, how long before you will judge and avenge our blood on those who dwell on the earth?" Then they were each given a white robe and told to rest a little longer, until the number of their fellow servants and their brothers should be

---

4. African American Spiritual, "Wade in the Water," *Evangelical Lutheran Worship* (Minneapolis: Augsburg Fortress, 2006), 459.

complete, who were to be killed as they themselves had been.

When he opened the sixth seal, I looked, and behold, there was a great earthquake, and the sun became black as sackcloth, the full moon became like blood, and the stars of the sky fell to the earth as the fig tree sheds its winter fruit when shaken by a gale. The sky vanished like a scroll that is being rolled up, and every mountain and island was removed from its place. Then the kings of the earth and the great ones and the generals and the rich and the powerful, and everyone, slave and free, hid themselves in the caves and among the rocks of the mountains, calling to the mountains and rocks, "Fall on us and hide us from the face of him who is seated on the throne, and from the wrath of the Lamb, for the great day of their wrath has come, and who can stand?" (Rev 6:9–17, italics mine)

About sixty years after these words were written, Polycarp, a resident of Smyrna (Rev 2:8–11), was martyred for being a Christian. When asked to deny his faith, Polycarp responded: "For eighty-six years have I served Christ and he has done me no wrong. How can I blaspheme my King and my Savior?"[5] Polycarp was a young man when Revelation was first read to the church in Smyrna. We don't know if he was there; however, we do know that his martyrdom inspired many Christians to hold fast to Christ in the face of persecution and oppression.

To be a martyr is to experience a violent death for one's faith. Revelation 20 speaks of martyrs who are beheaded for giving testimony of Jesus (Rev 20:4). By outward observations, martyrs might appear to be forsaken by God. However, in this vision, God cares for the martyrs by giving them white robes and telling them to rest. The gifts show that the martyrs are valued. They are the ones who have conquered, just as Jesus is the slain Lamb who conquers. This really is the answer to God's allowing the four riders to trample the ground upon which we live. Revelation tells us the four riders aren't the last word.

5. Gonzales, *Story of Christianity,* 54.

Over and against the martyrs, Revelation contrasts the inhabitants of the earth who place their trust in the things of the earth brought by the four riders (nations, peace, wealth, and health). By outward observations, the people have it good. They are, however, the ones whose lives are turned into chaos when everything they depended upon fails. The earth, moon, and stars are off course. The earth quakes. No military general, political leader, athlete, or celebrity can save them from doom. The situation is so horrific, Revelation 6 ends with a question that must be answered: "Who can stand?" Why of course, no one![6]

> From all that terror teaches,
> From lies of tongue and pen,
> From all the easy speeches
> That comfort cruel men,
> From sale and profanation
> Of honor, and the sword,
> From sleep and from damnation
> Deliver us, good Lord![7]

THE REDEEMED STAND

The breaking of the first six seals brings terror on the earth. All that is left is for the Lamb to break the seventh seal and finish the desolation. However, instead of terror, we find restraint as four angels hold back the four winds until the 144,000 are marked with a seal of protection and belonging.[8]

> After this I saw four angels standing at the four corners
> of the earth, holding back the four winds of the earth,
> that no wind might blow on earth or sea or against any
> tree. Then I saw another angel ascending from the rising

6. Peterson, *Reversed Thunder*, 64.

7. G. K. Chesterton, "O God of Earth and Altar," *Ancient and Modern: Hymns and Songs for Refreshing Worship* (London: Hymns Ancient & Modern, 2013), 582, verse 2.

8. Koester, *Revelation*, 416.

of the sun, with the seal of the living God, and he called with a loud voice to the four angels who had been given power to harm earth and sea, saying, "Do not harm the earth or the sea or the trees, until we have sealed the servants of our God on their foreheads." And I heard the number of the sealed, 144,000, sealed from every tribe of the sons of Israel: 12,000 from the tribe of Judah were sealed, 12,000 from the tribe of Reuben, 12,000 from the tribe of Gad, 12,000 from the tribe of Asher, 12,000 from the tribe of Naphtali, 12,000 from the tribe of Manasseh, 12,000 from the tribe of Simeon, 12,000 from the tribe of Levi, 12,000 from the tribe of Issachar, 12,000 from the tribe of Zebulun, 12,000 from the tribe of Joseph, 12,000 from the tribe of Benjamin were sealed. (Rev 7:1–8)

Who are the 144,000? Should we believe, as the Jehovah's Witnesses do, that literally only 144,000 people will be saved? Is this number symbolic? Most interpreters believe the numbering of the 144,000 is a symbolic census of the army of martyrs. In the Old Testament, a census was used to measure the military strength of the nation.[9] The symbolism is further developed by the next verse that speaks of a *Great Multitude* from every nation, tribe, and people group so vast that it cannot be counted. In other words, the "144,000" mentioned in v. 4 is the "Great Multitude" mentioned in v. 9. This might appear to be a contradiction until we remember earlier how John heard of the Lion of Judah (Rev 5:5) but saw the Lamb (Rev 5:6). In the same way, John *hears* about the 144,000 Israelites, but actually *sees* a Great Multitude of people who cannot be counted. By this, we learn that the faithful are made up of men, women, and children from every tribe and nation.[10]

After this I looked, and behold, a great multitude that no one could number, from every nation, from all tribes and peoples and languages, standing before the throne and before the Lamb, clothed in white robes, with palm branches in their hands, and crying out with a loud

9. Bauckham, *Theology of the Book of Revelation*, 77.
10. Koester, *Revelation and the End of All Things*, 90.

voice, "Salvation belongs to our God who sits on the throne, and to the Lamb!" And all the angels were standing around the throne and around the elders and the four living creatures, and they fell on their faces before the throne and worshiped God, saying, "Amen! Blessing and glory and wisdom and thanksgiving and honor and power and might be to our God forever and ever! Amen." (Rev 7:9–12)

Like Miriam who sang of God's triumph over Pharaoh's armies at the Red Sea in Exodus, the Great Multitude sings a song of salvation, which can be translated "victory."[11] They have joined the elders and flying creatures in praising God. Before we consider their posture, it is essential to note that the multitude is made up of people from every tribe and nation (Rev 7:9). This is multiculturalism at its finest and it is a vision of eternity as people will praise God in their native tongues.

As a college pastor, I was fortunate to take students to the Urbana—one of the largest student missions conferences in the world. At the conference, approximately 18,000 students from 80 countries gathered in the name of Christ. We sang songs in Arabic, Chinese, English, Hawaiian, and Spanish, It was one of the most powerful worship experiences of my life and it is a preview of what worship will be like in heaven. Until then, may we as a people strive to embrace each other!

As mentioned above, the posture of the Great Multitude is significant because they are "standing" (Rev 7:9). Earlier, it was assumed that no one could stand, because no one was worthy (Rev 6:17). The breaking open of the seventh seal has worked and the faithful stand! Now God establishes a new seal, a seal of faith on human hearts. As the apostle St. Paul writes, "And it is God who establishes us with you in Christ, and has anointed us, and who has also put his seal on us and given us his Spirit in our hearts as a guarantee" (2 Cor 1:21–22). We learn more about the Great Multitude in the following verses:

11. Caird, *Revelation of Saint John*, 100.

Then one of the elders addressed me, saying, "Who are these, clothed in white robes, and from where have they come?" I said to him, "Sir, you know." And he said to me, "These are the ones coming out of the great tribulation. They have washed their robes and made them white in the blood of the Lamb. "Therefore they are before the throne of God, and serve him day and night in his temple; and he who sits on the throne will shelter them with his presence. They shall hunger no more, neither thirst anymore; the sun shall not strike them, nor any scorching heat. For the Lamb in the midst of the throne will be their shepherd, and he will guide them to springs of living water, and God will wipe away every tear from their eyes." (Rev 7:13–17)

The description of the crowd is important. First, they wear white robes given to them by Christ (Rev 3:18). Second, they hold palm branches and celebrate the victory of the Lamb.[12] The Great Multitude can conquer in the midst of persecution because the Lamb is victorious over death. The point is clear: when the veneer of this world's false security is stripped away, left standing are Christians who are victorious because Jesus has them in hand.

When I saw my wife after school on 9/11, she looked exhausted. She used every ounce of her strength to get through the day. In fact, when I hugged her, she collapsed in my arms. I held her tight and wiped the tears from her face. As we have reflected on that day, two things stand out. First, she learned just how strong she is. Second, she learned that when her legs give way, Jesus is there to help her stand.

> *O happy day when we shall stand,*
> *Amid the heav'nly throne,*
> *And sing with hosts from ev'ry land*
> *The new celestial song,*
> *The new celestial song.*[13]

---

12. Koester, *Revelation*, 428.

13. Wilhelm A. Wexels, "O Happy Day When We Shall Stand," *Evangelical Lutheran Worship* (Minneapolis: Augsburg Fortress, 2006), 441, verse 1.

Refocus Questions

1. The four horsemen represent the things we trust above God (nation, civil peace, wealth, and health). In which of these things do you often place your trust? Why do you think you do it?

2. The four horsemen disturb the order of things. Do you like this idea or not? When is it necessary to disrupt the world? When is it better to be patient?

3. If you were faced with dying a martyr, do you think you would keep the faith? Why or why not? How does this vision of a martyr receiving the white robe give comfort?

4. The 144,000 / Great Multitude are marked with a seal of protection. How might the seal bring courage to the Christian?

5. The 144,000 / Great Multitude is a beautiful multicultural picture of heaven. In your own life, do you know people of different ethnic groups? Have you ever worshiped with them in their native tongue?

6. In your town or city, what is one way that you could engage another person from a different ethnic group?

7. The end of ch. 7 (Rev 7:15–17) mentions promises found in the Old Testament. How do these promises affirm the faithfulness of God? Are there any promises that you might hold onto from this list?

CYCLE 3

EVANGELISM

REVELATION 8–9

The Alarm Sounds

The rest of mankind, who were not killed by these plagues, did not repent of their murders or their sorceries or their sexual immorality of their thefts. (Rev 9:20–21)

IT MUST HAVE FELT like a dream, or rather a nightmare, for Jews living in Bulgaria during World War II. At 3:00 a.m. on March 10, 1943, police rounded up Bulgarian Jews and held them at the train station in Plovdiv, the second-largest city in Bulgaria. The next day, they would be sent by train to a concentration camp in Germany. Two years earlier, Bulgaria had signed the Tripartite Pact and became an ally of Nazi Germany. Even though restrictions and abuses were applied to the Jews living in Bulgaria, no one believed serious harm would come to Bulgaria's Jewish citizens. They were wrong; their fellow citizens faced certain extermination.

Thankfully, not everyone was asleep. A pastor, Metropolitan Kyril, saw what was happening and raised the alarm. Like a trumpet blast, his opposition voice called people to act. When Metropolitan Kyril received news of the round-up, he sprang into action and went down to the train station. He announced that if a train loaded with Jews tried to leave the city, he would lie across the railroad tracks. Guards removed him from the tracks, but this did not deter him. Defying the guards, he climbed the fence, jumped into the yard, and addressed the Jews who flocked around him. Quoting from the book of Ruth, he said, "Wherever you go—I'll go."[1] The act of this faithful man would save many lives.

Many first-century Christians living in Asia Minor were asleep. Even though some Christians faced persecution, many did not. In fact, numerous Christians were doing quite well for themselves. They had good jobs and made good money. Like the inhabitants of Laodicea earlier in Revelation, they had an abundance of gold, but none that had been refined by the fire of Christian witness (Rev 3:18). They were comfortable—a little too comfortable. They needed an alarm to wake them from their stupor.

THE TRUMPET SOUNDS

Revelation 8 begins with the words, "When the Lamb opened the seventh seal, there was silence in heaven for about half an hour" (Rev 8:1). This is a startling contrast to the opening of the previous seals that shook the earth. The silence is the opportunity to prepare the imagination to receive an incredible truth.[2] What truth will God reveal?

As we wait for our answer, John directs our attention to seven angels who are each handed a trumpet. God's people have a long history with trumpets. Trumpets were used in battle, used to introduce kings, and used during worship festivals. The walls of Jericho crumbled because of trumpets. Moses called and dismissed the people of Israel with two silver trumpets. Trumpets blasts even summoned Israel to national repentance (Jer 4:5; Ezek 33:3; Isa 58:1; Joel 2:1).[3] Search for "shofar" on the internet and the listener can hear the powerful blast of the horn that called the people to

---

1. Bar-Zohar, *Beyond Hitler's Grasp*, 126.
2. Peterson, *Reversed Thunder*, 87.
3. Caird, *Revelation of Saint John*, 108–11.

hear the Lord. It is no accident that the angels were given trumpets to awaken God's people to action.

> When the Lamb opened the seventh seal, there was silence in heaven for about half an hour. Then I saw the seven angels who stand before God, and seven trumpets were given to them. And another angel came and stood at the altar with a golden censer, and he was given much incense to offer with the prayers of all the saints on the golden altar before the throne, and the smoke of the incense, with the prayers of the saints, rose before God from the hand of the angel. Then the angel took the censer and filled it with fire from the altar and threw it on the earth, and there were peals of thunder, rumblings, flashes of lightning, and an earthquake. Now the seven angels who had the seven trumpets prepared to blow them.
>
> *The first angel blew his trumpet*, and there followed hail and fire, mixed with blood, and these were thrown upon the earth. And a third of the earth was burned up, and a third of the trees were burned up, and all green grass was burned up.
>
> *The second angel blew his trumpet*, and something like a great mountain, burning with fire, was thrown into the sea, and a third of the sea became blood. A third of the living creatures in the sea died, and a third of the ships were destroyed.
>
> *The third angel blew his trumpet*, and a great star fell from heaven, blazing like a torch, and it fell on a third of the rivers and on the springs of water. The name of the star is Wormwood. A third of the waters became wormwood, and many people died from the water, because it had been made bitter.
>
> *The fourth angel blew his trumpet*, and a third of the sun was struck, and a third of the moon, and a third of the stars, so that a third of their light might be darkened, and a third of the day might be kept from shining, and likewise a third of the night. (Rev 8:1–12, italics mine)

The first four trumpet blasts usher in a series of natural disasters very similar to the ten plagues mentioned in Egypt (Exod 7–12). After God raised Moses to be his mouthpiece to call Egypt to repentance, God sent signs and wonders to make it happen. Sadly, Pharaoh did not repent, but it didn't stop Moses from proclaiming his message.

Too often we lack Moses' tenacity. Dawson Trotman, founder of Navigators Ministry, did not give up. In the 1930s, Trotman, a young California lumberyard worker, decided to share his faith. He began teaching high school students. Often there was little fruit, but he kept proclaiming. In 1933, he and his friends extended their work to sailors in the US Navy. There, Dawson taught sailor Les Spencer about the Christian faith. They spent many hours together praying, studying God's Word, and memorizing Scripture. Eventually, God's work between these two extended to 125 men on the USS *West Virginia*, who grew in faith. By the end of World War II, thousands of men on ships and bases around the world were learning about the Christian faith. Dawson Trotman's faith kept him from giving up, and God's Word allowed those who heard it to navigate the difficult waters of war.[4]

We will have to wait until Revelation 11 to see God raise up another Moses to be a witness. Until then, our attention is drawn to a different messenger, namely, an eagle whose message is not good news, but rather, "Woe, woe, woe!"

> Then I looked, and I heard an eagle crying with a loud voice as it flew directly overhead, "Woe, woe, woe to those who dwell on the earth, at the blasts of the other trumpets that the three angels are about to blow!" *And the fifth angel blew his trumpet,* and I saw a star fallen from heaven to earth, and he was given the key to the shaft of the bottomless pit. He opened the shaft of the bottomless pit, and from the shaft rose smoke like the smoke of a great furnace, and the sun and the air were darkened with the smoke from the shaft. Then from the

4. Navigators, "Our History," http://www.navigators.org/About-Us/History.

smoke came locusts on the earth, and they were given power like the power of scorpions of the earth. They were told not to harm the grass of the earth or any green plant or any tree, but only those people who do not have the seal of God on their foreheads. They were allowed to torment them for five months, but not to kill them, and their torment was like the torment of a scorpion when it stings someone. And in those days people will seek death and will not find it. They will long to die, but death will flee from them. In appearance the locusts were like horses prepared for battle: on their heads were what looked like crowns of gold; their faces were like human faces, their hair like women's hair, and their teeth like lions' teeth; they had breastplates like breastplates of iron, and the noise of their wings was like the noise of many chariots with horses rushing into battle. They have tails and stings like scorpions, and their power to hurt people for five months is in their tails. They have as king over them the angel of the bottomless pit. His name in Hebrew is Abaddon, and in Greek he is called Apollyon. The first woe has passed; behold, two woes are still to come. (Rev 8:13—9:12, italics mine)

Passages like this one in Revelation cause fanciful speculation. Hal Lindsey wrote *The Late Great Planet Earth*, his interpretation of Revelation, in the midst of the Vietnam War and the unsettling cultural changes of the '60s and '70s. He supposed that the strange locusts in this chapter were attack helicopters. He believed the "crowns of gold" describe helmets that helicopter pilots wear. He thought the hair like "women's hair" likely referred to the whirling blades of a helicopter and the teeth "like lions' teeth" could mean the weapons that project from the helicopter.[5] During the Gulf War, many followers of Lindsey speculated that if the Vietnam War wasn't the end, then this would be it. But they were wrong. Lindsey and his followers are not the only ones to get it wrong. In 1986, when the Chernobyl nuclear accident occurred, many believed it was the fulfillment of Revelation 8:10–11 because

---

5. Lindsey, *Late Great Planet Earth*, 42.

"Chernobyl" in Russian is translated "wormwood." The nuclear accident poisoned the water and many died. Again, many speculated that this was the end of the world. Again, they were wrong.

William Miller, from whose preaching the Seventh Day Adventist movement came, believed the world would end in 1844 based on his calculations of Revelation. Charles Russell, founder of the Jehovah's Witness, believed the world would end in 1914. In each of these cases, and many others, the interpreters tried to order the events of Revelation into a coherent timeline and then connect the timeline to contemporary news. In each and every case, they were wrong. In our own lives, we often face circumstances like sickness, deaths of loved ones, or financial disaster that make us think we can't go on. We, too, think that this is the end of life as we know it, but we're as wrong as the others were.

There is another way to read these words from Revelation: instead of reading them as a prescriptive of future events, read them for the truth they convey. As Craig Koester explains, "The judgment depicted here is not direct divine punishment, but a revelation of what it would mean for God to hand over the world to other powers."[6] Clearly, God is not going to hand over the world. However, the warning of the seven seals (Rev 6), seven trumpets (Rev 8), and seven bowls (Rev 16) is directed at Christians who are not fighting against the evils of their day. Christians are marked by the Spirit. Christians are secure because they conquer through the blood of the Lamb. To fail to act is to deny the very power a Christian has and is utter disaster to those who do not yet believe.

NOR DID THEY REPENT . . .

God has not handed the world over to the enemy. The real question is whether we have. Before we can answer, the next trumpet sounds and the second woe occurs.

---

6. Koester, *Revelation and the End of All Things*, 100.

Then the sixth angel blew his trumpet, and I heard a voice
from the four horns of the golden altar before God, saying to the sixth angel who had the trumpet, "Release the
four angels who are bound at the great river Euphrates."
So the four angels, who had been prepared for the hour,
the day, the month, and the year, were released to kill a
third of mankind. The number of mounted troops was
twice ten thousand times ten thousand; I heard their
number. And this is how I saw the horses in my vision
and those who rode them: they wore breastplates the
color of fire and of sapphire and of sulfur, and the heads
of the horses were like lions' heads, and fire and smoke
and sulfur came out of their mouths. By these three
plagues a third of mankind was killed, by the fire and
smoke and sulfur coming out of their mouths. For the
power of the horses is in their mouths and in their tails,
for their tails are like serpents with heads, and by means
of them they wound. The rest of mankind, who were not
killed by these plagues, did not repent of the works of
their hands nor give up worshiping demons and idols of
gold and silver and bronze and stone and wood, which
cannot see or hear or walk, nor did they repent of their
murders or their sorceries or their sexual immorality or
their thefts. (Rev 9:13–21, italics mine)

A mighty cavalry of monsters is released. Much like the
Uruk-hai, the vile orc hybrids that serve the evil enemy in the *Lord
of the Rings*, these animals are a demonic blend: part horse, part
lion, and part serpent.[7] They wreak havoc on the earth. Surely with
such destruction from demonic forces the people would repent
and return to God, but they don't. As the last verse says, "Nor did
they repent . . ." (Rev 9:21). Clearly, the horrors of judgment did
not move the surviving inhabitants to repent of worshiping demons and idols of gold and silver. This is crucial. Judgment alone
will not lead to repentance, and the demands of God's law in the
Commandments don't change hearts.[8] Plagues did not convert the

7. Caird, *Revelation of Saint John*, 122.

8. Bauckham, *Theology of the Book of Revelation*, 86.

people of Egypt. Plagues will not convert the people of this world. If Christians abdicate their responsibility in loving the people of this world, the only result will be faithlessness. We, as Christians, must wake up. The trumpet is sounding. The alarm is going off.

When Metropolitan Kyril stood up for the Bulgarian Jews, he caught the attention Bulgaria's King Boris. From the outset, Boris had been hesitant to align with Hitler but reluctantly allowed the abuse of Jews to occur. Thankfully, the actions of Metropolitan Kyril created courage within Boris, who released the Jews in the train station on March 11, 1943. Hitler would not get his hands on the Bulgarian Jews. Bulgaria would be the only Axis power that refused to send its Jewish citizens to Hitler.[9] That is what happens when God's people are awake to the needs of this world. The alarm is sounding. Are we awake?

> *Jesus gave the mandate;*
> *Share the good news*
> *That he came to save us*
> *And set us free.*
>
> *Listen, listen, God is calling*
> *Through the word inviting,*
> *Offering forgiveness,*
> *comfort and joy.*[10]

---

9. Bar-Zohar, *Beyond Hitler's Grasp*, 113ff.

10. Tanzanian Traditional, "Listen, Listen, God Is Calling," *Evangelical Lutheran Worship* (Minneapolis: Augsburg Fortress, 2006), 513, verse 1 with refrain.

Refocus Questions

1. Describe a time when someone stuck his or her neck out for you or when you did it for someone else? How did you feel in that moment? How did it impact you in the long run?

2. In the passage (Rev 9:4), we learn that the Christians who have a seal on the forehead will be safe. How do these words comfort you? How do these words inspire you to act?

3. As Christians, it is easy to relax because our future is secure. What is the cost of not engaging the world?

4. How does the reference to plagues (Rev 8:7–12) help you understand the importance of taking sides on matters? What are some plagues occurring in our world today that we should address?

5. As in every age, there is clearly evil occurring in the world today. Why do you think so many people are asleep in handling it? What do you think can wake them up? What has awakened you?

6. Why do you think so many people did not repent based on the destruction the alarm warns of in Revelation 9:21? If God's wrath does not change hearts, what will?

7. How would your community change if Christians engaged with this world's evils?

REVELATION 10–11

Will You Answer the Call?

And at that hour there was a great earthquake, and a tenth of the city fell. Seven thousand people were killed in the earthquake, and the rest were terrified and gave glory to the God of heaven. (Rev 11:13)

DURING SEMINARY, I WAS called into the campus pastor's office because of a prayer I said. Yes, I am serious. It was during the month of Ramadan, Islam's holy month of prayer and fasting. During our chapel service, I asked God to help Muslims see that Jesus Christ is Lord. As you might imagine, at a mainstream Protestant seminary, that prayer had strong reactions. A dozen "progressive" students were so offended by my prayer that I was called into the campus pastor's office to apologize. I refused to apologize because I did not do anything wrong. The conservative students loved my prayer because they believed it was an attack on political correctness; it was not. There was a third reaction, however, that took me by surprise.

Immediately after the service, many African students met me by the altar and kissed me on the cheek. With tears on their faces, they thanked me for offering such a prayer. Their affection was not due to politics or political correctness; it was something deeper. It was about faith. These students knew how difficult it is to offer such a prayer. They knew that I was making a public declaration of the Lordship of Jesus. They knew this made me vulnerable. They knew there might be consequences. They also knew that Jesus Christ is Lord. Their embrace was their way of saying "Amen!" to my prayer.

For Christians living in Asia Minor, they knew the consequences of saying, "Jesus is Lord!" It cost them business, friendships, and for some, their very lives. Why would any sane person make such a claim? Revelation 10 and 11 give us the answer.

TAKE AND EAT

In Revelation 8 and 9, we witnessed six trumpet blasts that ushered destruction upon the earth. The sad news was that, despite the judgment, no one repented (Rev 9:20). What is God to do with an unrepentant people? We witness God's response as an angel descends from heaven wrapped in a cloud, his voice like a lion causing seven thunders to sound. By all appearances, this is the end for an unbelieving people. We anxiously wait for the seventh trumpet to sound.

> Then I saw another mighty angel coming down from heaven, wrapped in a cloud, with a rainbow over his head, and his face was like the sun, and his legs like pillars of fire. He had a little scroll open in his hand. And he set his right foot on the sea, and his left foot on the land, and called out with a loud voice, like a lion roaring. When he called out, the seven thunders sounded. And when the seven thunders had sounded, I was about to write, but I heard a voice from heaven saying, "Seal up what the seven thunders have said, and do not write it down." And the angel whom I saw standing on the sea and on the land raised his right hand to heaven and swore by him who lives forever and ever, who created heaven and what is in it, the earth and what is in it, and the sea and what is in it, that there would be no more delay, but that in the days of the trumpet call to be sounded by the seventh

angel, the mystery of God would be fulfilled, just as he
announced to his servants the prophets. (Rev 10:1–7)

The seventh trumpet does not sound. There is a reprieve.
The angel, whose appearance is filled with authority—wrapped in
a cloud, face like the sun, and legs like pillars of fire—also has a
rainbow over his head. The rainbow, which like the earlier mention
of in Revelation is an allusion to the covenant God made with
Noah (Gen 9:13–16). It is a symbol that the storm has halted. With
this reprieve, the angel gives John an open scroll. The fact that
the scroll is "open" reminds us of the scroll opened by the Lamb
(Rev 5–8).[1] The fact that it is an angel who gives John the scroll reminds
us of Revelation 1:1: "The revelation of Jesus Christ, which
God gave him to show to his servants the things that must soon
take place. He made it known *by sending his angel to his servant
John.*" Could it be that John is given the very scroll that the Lamb
opened? Might this scroll be the very revelation of Jesus Christ?
While scholars differ on their answers to these questions, what is
certain is that God has now given humanity some time and has
given John the scroll so that the message would be shared and faith
would be strengthened.

> Then the voice that I had heard from heaven spoke to me
> again, saying, "Go, take the scroll that is open in the hand
> of the angel who is standing on the sea and on the land."
> So I went to the angel and told him to give me the little
> scroll. And he said to me, "Take and eat it; it will make
> your stomach bitter, but in your mouth it will be sweet as
> honey." And I took the little scroll from the hand of the
> angel and ate it. It was sweet as honey in my mouth, but
> when I had eaten it my stomach was made bitter. And I
> was told, "You must again prophesy about many peoples
> and nations and languages and kings." (Rev 10:8–11)

1. Richard Bauckham argues that "a major key to the correct interpretation
of Revelation has been missed by almost all scholars" because they fail to connect
"the scroll which John sees, sealed with seven seals, in the hand of God in
5:1 as the same open scroll in the hand of the angel in 10:2." Bauckham, *Climax
of Prophecy*, 243–54.

John is given the scroll to eat. Like the prophets Ezekiel and Jeremiah, John is called to eat the Word of God (see fig. 5). Eugene Boring explains the importance of eating the scroll by saying, "John is not merely a spectator and reporter of this scene; he becomes a main character, for the opened book in the hand of the mighty angel is meant for him."[2] Eugene Peterson suggests that such consumption gives "meaning, plot, and purpose" to life because eating the scroll means we "assimilate it into our very being."[3] When John eats the scroll, he experiences two things. First, it is sweet as candy. Second, it makes for some gastrointestinal distress. The message of the scroll is sweet because it is the gospel, but it is bitter because sharing the gospel often leads to suffering (and sometimes death) for God's witnesses.[4]

On Good Friday, April 3, 2015, Pope Francis, along with many other Christian leaders, renounced a recent wave of Christian persecution. A day earlier, terrorists entered a Kenyan school where they asked children and young adults if they were Christian or Muslim. The captives who were Muslim or willing to convert to Islam were spared. Those who held to their Christian faith were executed. On that day, 147 people were executed.[5] These young people were willing to experience real bitterness for the cause of Christ. Thankfully, they also received the sweetness of reigning with Jesus Christ, who overcame the grave and holds the keys to death (Rev 1:18). This is what makes him worthy (Rev 5:9). This promise is what these brave martyrs now fully know.

> For all the saints who from their labors rest,
> Who Thee by faith before the world confess,
> Thy name, O Jesus, be forever blest,
> Alleluia! Alleluia!

---

2. Boring, *Revelation*, 141.

3. Peterson, "Eat This Book," 1.

4. Koester, *Revelation and the End of All Things*, 104.

5. San Martín, "*On Good Friday*," 1.

XI

Description (Figure 5): John is given a book to eat. This is very similar to the prophet Ezekiel who also ate a scroll (Ezek 2:8–11). The book is sweet as honey at first, but then turns his stomach bitter. The sweetness is the gospel. The bitterness is the persecution that comes from sharing the faith.

Thou wast their Rock, their Fortress, and their Might;
Thou, Lord, their Captain in the well-fought fight;
Thou, in the darkness drear, their one true Light.
Alleluia! Alleluia![6]

CAN I GET A WITNESS?

Earlier in this chapter, God provided extra time so many could come to faith. Next, the angel gave John a scroll to devour. Now, the angel gives John a measuring rod to measure the temple of God and the altar of those who worship there.

> Then I was given a measuring rod like a staff, and I was told, "Rise and measure the temple of God and the altar and those who worship there, but do not measure the court outside the temple; leave that out, for it is given over to the nations, and they will trample the holy city for forty-two months." (Rev 11:1–2)

Many people have interpreted these words in a literal manner to insist that a third temple in Jerusalem must be rebuilt in our age and sacrifices must occur before the second coming of Jesus can occur. People who hold this view know that major obstacles are Muslim holy sites (the Dome of the Rock and the Al-Aqsa Mosque on the Temple Mount in Jerusalem) that occupy the place where Israel's third temple should be. This has caused all kinds of speculation as to how the third temple could once again be erected. In 1984, members of the "Jewish Underground" terror group planned to blow up these Muslim holy sites on the Temple Mount to make room for Israel's temple. Others believe a natural act of God will create space for the third temple to be built. No matter how they think it will happen, holders of this position are waiting for a physical temple to be constructed.

---

6. William How, "For All the Saints," *Lutheran Book of Worship* (Minneapolis: Augsburg, 1979), 174, verses 1 and 2 with refrain.

Readers of Revelation should take care to read these words in the context of the whole book of Revelation. For instance, "temple" and "holy city" are used as metaphors in the book of Revelation for the Christian community. Earlier in Revelation 3:12, the faithful were promised to be made into the pillars of the "temple" and that they would be named for God's own "city." Clearly, the faithful are not literal bricks and stones to be used for constructing a building. Rather, their witness is the very building blocks of the "temple" and "holy city." The point in this passage is not a literal building but rather the community that is built up by the proclamation of the gospel. John is measuring a *great temple* because God is sending witnesses to proclaim the *great message.*[7]

> "And I will grant authority to my two witnesses, and they will prophesy for 1,260 days, clothed in sackcloth." These are the two olive trees and the two lampstands that stand before the Lord of the earth. And if anyone would harm them, fire pours from their mouth and consumes their foes. If anyone would harm them, this is how he is doomed to be killed. They have the power to shut the sky, that no rain may fall during the days of their prophesying, and they have power over the waters to turn them into blood and to strike the earth with every kind of plague, as often as they desire. And when they have finished their testimony, the beast that rises from the bottomless pit will make war on them and conquer them and kill them, and their dead bodies will lie in the street of the great city that symbolically is called Sodom and Egypt, where their Lord was crucified. For three and a half days some from the peoples and tribes and languages and nations will gaze at their dead bodies and refuse to let them be placed in a tomb, and those who dwell on the earth will rejoice over them and make merry and exchange presents, because these two prophets had been a torment to those who dwell on the earth. (Rev 11:3–10)

7. Bauckham, *Theology of the Book of Revelation*, 84.

Two witnesses are sent out from God just as the disciples were sent out in pairs by Jesus (Mark 6:7; Luke 10:1). These two witness are much like Jesus' conversation partners in the story of the transfiguration, the prophets Elijah and Moses who had the authority to call down fire from heaven (1 Kgs 19:14–18) as well as turn water into blood (Exod 7:14–24). Neither Moses nor Elijah suffered martyrdom during their lives, but they did suffer greatly for their witness. As we saw earlier, the Greek word for "witness" is the same word for "martyr." For these two witnesses, as well as anyone who is a witness of the gospel, persecution will occur. Jesus promised this: "Servants are not greater than their master. If they persecuted me, they will persecute you" (John 15:20).

These two witnesses are persecuted and killed. Remember, the scroll that John ate was both sweet and bitter (Rev 10:10). However, God vindicates them and raises them from the dead. As a result of their witness, the majority of the city is converted.[8]

> But after the three and a half days a breath of life from God entered them, and they stood up on their feet, and great fear fell on those who saw them. Then they heard a loud voice from heaven saying to them, "Come up here!" And they went up to heaven in a cloud, and their enemies watched them. And at that hour there was a great earthquake, and a tenth of the city fell. Seven thousand people were killed in the earthquake, and the rest were terrified and gave glory to the God of heaven. The second woe has passed; behold, the third woe is soon to come. (Rev 11:11–14)

All but seven thousand people come to faith in God. Earlier, no one in the city believed. Destruction and judgment could not cause people to repent (Rev 9:20). Only the gospel creates faith. As the Apostle Paul says, "How are they to call on the one in whom they have not believed? And how are they to believe in one whom they have never heard? And how are they to hear without some to proclaim him? And how are they to proclaim him unless they are

---

8. Bauckham, *Theology of the Book of Revelation*, 86.

sent? As it is written, 'How beautiful are the feet of those who bring good news'" (Rom 10:14–15). The task of those sent is to tell others of God's promise in Christ.

On January 8, 1956, Jim Elliot, along with four of his missionary colleagues, attempted to establish contact with the Auca Indians in Ecuador, now known as the Waodani people. These five missionaries were young, educated, and talented. They were married and had young families. They desired to bring Christ to these natives, but instead of finding success, they were speared to death by the very people they were trying to reach. Their deaths were not in vain. Two years later, in October 1958, Elliot's wife, along with her three-year-old daughter Valerie and another woman, Elizabeth Saint, went to live with the very people who had killed their husbands. Their act of faith led to the conversion of the Waodani people. These women personally knew the bitterness of the gospel, but also its sweetness.[9]

Who taught you about Jesus? For me, it was my pastor Phil Tukua. Phil is unique. He isn't just a pastor, he is an evangelist. He is not afraid to share the gospel with a waiter, grocery checker, neighbor, or even a young sixteen-year-old boy looking for meaning and purpose in life and wanting to impress a Christian girl he met. I am glad Phil did not keep quiet. I am glad that he was willing to share the gospel. If he had not answered the call to evangelize, my life would not be the same. Thankfully, Phil gave me the Word of God to consume. In my life, I have tasted the bitterness of rejection, but I have also discovered there is nothing sweeter than seeing a person come to faith.

> *How sweet the Name of Jesus sounds*
> *In a believer's ear!*
> *It soothes his sorrows, heals his wounds,*
> *And drives away his fear.*
> *It makes the wounded spirit whole,*
> *And calms the troubled breast;*
> *'Tis manna to the hungry soul,*
> *And to the weary, rest.*[10]

---

9. Elliot, *Through Gates of Splendor.*

10. John Newton, "How Sweet the Name of Jesus Sounds," *Evangelical*

Refocus Questions

1. The scroll (which is the gospel) is both sweet and bitter. What are some of the sweet parts of the gospel?

2. What are some of the bitter parts of the gospel? What is hard about following Jesus?

3. We read that there is a delay in the last trumpet blowing. In 2 Peter 3:9, we hear that God is slow to his promise because he wants more people to be saved. Do you like this? Why?

4. Is there anyone you know who is not a Christian? Have you ever talked to that person about Jesus?

5. What scares you about sharing this message? What is the worst thing that might happen to you?

6. How might the life of Elizabeth Elliot inspire you to act?

7. Who taught you about Jesus? Whom have you taught?

Lutheran Worship (Minneapolis: Augsburg Fortress, 2006), 620, verses 1 and 2.

REVELATION 12–13

The Battle Rages

Now the salvation and the power and the kingdom of our God and the
authority of his Christ have come, for the accuser of our brothers has
been thrown down, who accuses them day and night before our God.

(Rev 12:10)

THE OLD HYMN "ONWARD Christian Soldiers" is built on the as-
sumption that we are in a war. This might seem strange to hear.
It's distasteful to some today that this once-beloved hymn has
been eliminated from many hymnals. So many of us rightfully
have been taught that the heart of Christianity is love: "For God so
loved the world, that he gave his only Son, that whoever believes
in him should not perish but have eternal life" (John 3:16). War
seems to be the opposite of love. It is not, however much it seems
like it is. As a result, Christians do not really know how to handle
military language. We wonder if hymns like this one or "Lift High
the Cross" are appropriate for worship. Many preachers even steer
clear of battle language.

In some ways, the shift away from military language is good.
In the past, military imagery has been used to advance vicious

political and national ideologies. However, military metaphors can be useful in understanding faith. Theologian Sarah Hinlicky Wilson explains, "Faith means war—not against the frail bodies of our brothers and sisters made in the image of God but against the sin within and the powers without."[1] Military language assumes a battle. There are clashes in this world that must be fought: class struggle, human trafficking, addiction, exploitation of the poor, and many more. Think of those caught up in the sex trade. They are prisoners of war and need liberation from their captors. Even Jesus used that same military language in his very first sermon when he promised to "liberate the captives and the oppressed" (Luke 3:18).

A great battle occurs between God and the devil in the second half of Revelation. In the war, the major warriors for evil include the beast, the false prophet, the harlot, and many hideous creatures. In such a battle, the temptation is to stay on the sideline and be a spectator like the crowds who traveled out of Washington to observe the carnage from a Virginia hill looking over the First Battle of Bull Run in the American Civil War. Revelation will not let us do that. Everyone must choose a side. The good news is that God wins this battle. The difficult news is that we have been drafted to fight.

THE ACCUSER IS CAST OUT

Revelation 12 begins with eyes directed to the sky. John sees a woman clothed with the sun and moon, wearing a crown of twelve stars. This majestic woman is pregnant with a child who is to rule the nations (see Ps 2:9). The child is Jesus. Though his birth should be celebrated, it is not, for danger looms as a great dragon is seeking to devour him. You can tell the dragon's intention of claiming authority by the seven diadems he wears. It wants to be seen as the ruler of all and thus wears the diadems.[2] Standing in its way is the child.

---

1. Wilson, "Peace, Peace, When There Is No Peace," 3–6.
2. Koester, *Revelation*, 545.

> And a great sign appeared in heaven: a woman clothed
> with the sun, with the moon under her feet, and on her
> head a crown of twelve stars. She was pregnant and was
> crying out in birth pains and the agony of giving birth.
> And another sign appeared in heaven: behold, a great
> red dragon, with seven heads and ten horns, and on
> his heads seven diadems. His tail swept down a third of
> the stars of heaven and cast them to the earth. And the
> dragon stood before the woman who was about to give
> birth, so that when she bore her child he might devour
> it. She gave birth to a male child, one who is to rule all
> the nations with a rod of iron, but her child was caught
> up to God and to his throne, and the woman fled into the
> wilderness, where she has a place prepared by God, in
> which she is to be nourished for 1,260 days. (Rev 12:1–6)

The dragon waits with anticipation to devour Jesus (Rev 12:4). Thankfully, once Jesus is born, God intervenes and takes him to heaven (Rev 12:5). In the split-second interval between his birth and rescue in this picture, the book of Revelation compresses the entire life and ministry of Jesus: birth, ministry, passion, death, resurrection, and ascension.[3] What is important is not how Revelation tells history, but rather the immediate consequence of Jesus' birth. Instead of Christmas carols being sung and the happy exchange of gifts, a great war spreads across the heavens.[4]

> Now war arose in heaven, Michael and his angels fight-
> ing against the dragon. And the dragon and his angels
> fought back, but he was defeated, and there was no lon-
> ger any place for them in heaven. And the great dragon
> was thrown down, that ancient serpent, who is called the
> devil and Satan, the deceiver of the whole world—he was
> thrown down to the earth, and his angels were thrown
> down with him. And I heard a loud voice in heaven, say-
> ing, "Now the salvation and the power and the kingdom
> of our God and the authority of his Christ have come, for

3. Louis Brighton explains that the entire earthly ministry of Christ is compressed into the words, "snatched up to God." Brighton, *Revelation*, 331.

4. Peterson, *Reverse Thunder*, 120.

the accuser of our brothers has been thrown down, who accuses them day and night before our God. And they have conquered him by the blood of the Lamb and by the word of their testimony, for they loved not their lives even unto death. Therefore, rejoice, O heavens and you who dwell in them! But woe to you, O earth and sea, for the devil has come down to you in great wrath, because he knows that his time is short!" (Rev 12:7–12)

Satan loses the war in heaven and is cast out (see fig. 6). The Greek word for "cast out" can be translated "bounced."[5] Think about this word in context. The archangel Michael is like a bouncer at a bar who kicks the dragon out of the party. As a result, the dragon has been shut out. In this case, the dragon, who is the great accuser of God's people, no longer has access to God (Rev 12:10). In other words, the dragon cannot accuse us like it accused Job (Job 1:6–12). The dragon has been kicked out, shut out, and denied entrance. It has no avenue to carry its accusations of us to God. Michael is there denying entry at every turn. So when we begin to feel the accusation that we haven't been good enough or religious enough, or that God couldn't possibly care for us, the accusations we feel bearing down on us are no longer to be taken seriously. By being bounced, the prophet Isaiah's vision of the dragon is fulfilled:

How you are fallen from heaven, O Day Star, son of Dawn! How you are cut down to the ground, you who laid the nations low! You said in your heart, "I will ascend to heaven; above the stars of God." . . . But you are brought down to Sheol, to the far reaches of the pit. (Isa 14:12–15)

Many years ago, a young woman walked into my church office. She was member of the church and she wanted to talk. She sat down and said, "I have sex for money. I am a prostitute." Saying those very words made her sob. She had never said those words out loud. At that moment, she felt the weight of her actions. She

5. Ibid.

St. Michael Fighting the Dragon by Albrecht Dürer

XIII

Description (Figure 6): St. Michael casts out (or bounces) Satan from heaven.

immediately heard the devil's accusation. It told her that her identity was "prostitute." But remember, the devil cannot carry such accusations to God. The devil may be able to sling them our way, but the dragon has no access to God. Knowing this, I looked at her and said, "No, you are a child of God. That is who you are!" Hearing those words changed her. God's claim on her life gave her a new identity and a new hope. She began to see herself the way that God sees her. After continued conversation and follow up, she decided to move back home and has received support from her family.

The accuser has been bounced. The Evil One can bring his accusations to us, but he cannot bring them to God. That is why the Apostle Paul can say: "There is therefore now no condemnation for those who are in Christ Jesus" (Rom 8:1).

AN UNLIKELY ALLY

The defeat of the dragon (Rev 12:7–9) is the same event as the victory of the Lamb (Rev 5:5–6).[6] With its defeat, the dragon turns its focus to the earth. At first glance, this is terrifying for the earth: "But woe to you, O earth and sea, for the devil has come down to you in great wrath, because he knows that his time is short!" (Rev 12:12). It is the last phrase that gives us a glimmer of hope. It says the dragon's time "is short." Satan's rule is limited. He has lost territory (he can longer access heaven) and has lost run out of time to act (his time will end). Craig Koester explains the significance of this: "Those who think that Satan rages because he is invincible will give up in despair, but those who recognize that Satan rages on earth because he has already lost heaven and is now desperate have reason to resist him, confident that God will prevail."[7] Satan sets his fury against the woman and all her offspring not because he is invincible, but rather because he wants to inflict as much harm as possible before he is destroyed.[8]

---

6. Bauckham, *Climax of Prophecy*, 185–98.
7. Koester, *Revelation and the End of All Things*, 123.
8. Brighton, *Revelation*, 339.

And when the dragon saw that he had been thrown down to the earth, he pursued the woman who had given birth to the male child. But the woman was given the two wings of the great eagle so that she might fly from the serpent into the wilderness, to the place where she is to be nourished for a time, and times, and half a time. The serpent poured water like a river out of his mouth after the woman, to sweep her away with a flood. But the earth came to the help of the woman, and the earth opened its mouth and swallowed the river that the dragon had poured from his mouth. Then the dragon became furious with the woman and went off to make war on the rest of her offspring, on those who keep the commandments of God and hold to the testimony of Jesus. And he stood on the sand of the sea. (Rev 12:13–17)

Though the child is safe with God, the woman is vulnerable in the wilderness. Who is this woman? One would naturally assume it is Mary; however, it says the woman is the mother of many "offspring" who "keep the commandments of God and hold the testimony of Jesus." In typical Revelation fashion, the imagery is broad. The woman is not simply Mary, Israel, the church, or Eve. Rather, it is a combination of all of these.[9] Remember, Eve is the mother of all the living (Gen 3:16). The people of Israel spent time in the wilderness and passed through the waters of the Red Sea (Exod 15). The church is the bride of Christ (Rev 19:7–9). The story of the woman and her descendants is really the story of God's people. By combining these various aspects of the biblical narrative, John is helping us see that it is our story as well.

As Christians we live in the wilderness. We are sojourners. We do not get our best life now. While we wait for eternity, the dragon tries to harm us. And so we must fight. As the Apostle Paul argues, we rage "not against flesh and blood but against the rulers, against the authorities, against the cosmic powers over this present darkness, against the spiritual forces of evil in the heavenly places" (Eph 6:12).

9. Boring, *Revelation*, 152.

We read that the dragon sent forth a mighty flood into the wilderness, hoping to destroy the people of God (Rev 12:15). Thankfully, an unlikely ally comes to the rescue. The earth opens up to swallow the flood, thus saving the woman (Rev 12:16). Why would the earth do this? We have inflicted great harm on creation through deforestation, pollution, fracking, greenhouse gases, etc. If anything, creation should fight against us. It doesn't because creation belongs to the Creator. Creation stands in solidarity with us, because we and Creation both wait for redemption (Rom 8:19).[10] Our promised future is creation's future as well. The hope of Easter for us is the resurrection of the dead while the hope of Easter for creation is a renewal of the earth. If there is ever a reason for conservation it is this.

> All creatures of our God and King,
> lift up your voices, let us sing:
> Alleluia, alleluia!
> Thou burning sun with golden beams,
> thou silver moon that gently gleams,
> O praise him, O praise him,
> Alleluia, alleluia, alleluia![11]

THE FIRST BEAST: ENEMY FROM THE SEA

Though the dragon's days are numbered it continues to bring destruction on the earth. In ch. 13, we see it launch a new attack through two beasts: one from the sea and the other from land. The first amphibious attack comes from a hideous beast of the sea. The word "sea" can be translated "abyss" or "hell."[12] This beast comes from hell, the place of punishment, torment and eternal accusation.

---

10. Haught, *"Christianity and Ecology,"* 232ff.

11. Francis of Assisi, "All Creatures of Our God and King," *Lutheran Book of Worship* (Minneapolis: Augsburg, 1979), 527, verse 1.

12. Brighton, *Revelation*, 348.

And he [the dragon] stood on the sand of the sea. And I saw a beast rising out of the sea, with ten horns and seven heads, with ten diadems on its horns and blasphemous names on its heads. And the beast that I saw was like a leopard; its feet were like a bear's, and its mouth was like a lion's mouth. And to it the dragon gave his power and his throne and great authority. One of its heads seemed to have a mortal wound, but its mortal wound was healed, and the whole earth marveled as they followed the beast. And they worshiped the dragon, for he had given his authority to the beast, and they worshiped the beast, saying, "Who is like the beast, and who can fight against it?" And the beast was given a mouth uttering haughty and blasphemous words, and it was allowed to exercise authority for forty-two months. It opened its mouth to utter blasphemies against God, blaspheming his name and his dwelling, that is, those who dwell in heaven. Also it was allowed to make war on the saints and to conquer them. And authority was given it over every tribe and people and language and nation, and all who dwell on earth will worship it, everyone whose name has not been written before the foundation of the world in the book of life of the Lamb who was slain. If anyone has an ear, let him hear: If anyone is to be taken captive, to captivity he goes; if anyone is to be slain with the sword, with the sword must he be slain. Here is a call for the endurance and faith of the saints. (Rev 12:17b—13:10)

The first beast is hideous. Like the monstrous creature assembled from pieces of cadavers by Frankenstein, the first beast is pieced together—part leopard, bear, and with ten horns on its head. The purpose of this monster is to deceive. It is created to be like the Lamb with the sole purpose of causing people to worship the dragon (Rev 13:8).[13] Compare and contrast the beast with the Lamb:

---

13. Boring, *Revelation*, 156.

The Beast	The Lamb
Authority from the Dragon (Rev 13:2)	Authority from God (Rev 5:12–13)
Slain yet lives (Rev 13:3)	Slain yet lives (Rev 5:6)
Rules for a short time (Rev 13:5)	Rules for eternity (Rev 11:15)
Conquers by war (Rev 13:7)	Conquers by sacrifice (Rev 5:5)
Oppresses people of every tribe (Rev 13:7)	Ransoms people of every tribe (Rev 5:9)[14]

With the arrival of the beast, readers are drawn into the conflict. Neutrality is no longer possible. Either a person will worship God or worship the dragon. There is great pressure to simply give into the beast. It is grotesque. It is powerful. It causes the multitude to say, "Who is like the beast, and who can fight against it?" (Rev 13:4).

Margo, a member of my congregation, knew what it was like to fight such a beast. Margo was born in Germany and was a young woman living there during World War II. As a girl, Margo decided to place her Christian faith above the Nazi Party. Yet as a German citizen, she also could not escape the war. Her sister died from a bombing raid by the Allies. Margo's husband was shipped off in the German army to fight the Russians. In all the carnage and loss, Margo lost her faith. How could she stand in the face of such monstrosities?

After the bombing, Margo was assigned to lead German children out of Germany into Yugoslavia. One day, as the children camped, Margo came across a tiny chapel. She could hear someone practicing the organ. She walked into the chapel and sat down. Hearing the music, she began to weep. She wept over the loss of her sister and the pain of the past few years of war. She also wept tears of joy because she knew God had not abandoned her. She knew that she could stand. In that tiny chapel, her faith was renewed. Though the monstrosities of evil had dampened her faith, they could not extinguish it. Margo knew that she might continue

14. Koester, *Revelation and the End of All Things*, 127.

to suffer in this world, but she would overcome the world because she was united to Christ (John 16:33).

John's vision tells us that the beast will reign for forty-two months. We have heard this number in different ways throughout Revelation: forty-two months (Rev 11:2; 13:15); 1,260 days (Rev 11:3, 12:6); and three and a half years (Rev 12:4). In each of these cases, the time does not refer to a literal period of time. Rather, it signifies the fact that in every age, God's people will suffer. But, just as the dragon's time is limited, so too is the beast's. The suffering will end.[15]

The hope for God's people is to endure, for their names are written in the "book of life of the Lamb who was slain" (Rev 13:8). Earlier in Revelation 3:5, we learned about the book of life. What is significant is the additional descriptor: "book of life *of the Lamb who was slain.*" This is the key. The Lamb knows suffering. The Lamb was slain. But the Lamb overcame and holds the keys to death and hades. The Lamb has the real power. His reign does not last a mere forty-two months, but lasts forever. This is the truth that Margo discovered. Though she suffered greatly, she endured. Her name is written in the Lamb's book of life.

> *Now into your heart we pour*
> *Prayers that from our hearts proceeded.*
> *Our petitions heavenward soar;*
> *May our heart's desire be heeded!*
> *Write the name we now have given;*
> *Write it in the book of heaven!*[16]

THE SECOND BEAST: ENEMY FROM THE LAND

The first beast is followed by a second that rises out of the earth. Like its sibling, the second beast exercises authority to cause false

---

15. Koester, *Revelation*, 585.

16. Benjamin Schmolck, "Dearest Jesus, We Are Here," *Lutheran Book of Worship* (Minneapolis: Augsburg, 1979), 187, verse 5.

worship. In fact, this beast uses fire and false signs to lead people astray. One could say this beast is the antithesis of the two witnesses mentioned in Revelation 11.

> Then I saw another beast rising out of the earth. It had two horns like a lamb and it spoke like a dragon. It exercises all the authority of the first beast in its presence, and makes the earth and its inhabitants worship the first beast, whose mortal wound was healed. It performs great signs, even making fire come down from heaven to earth in front of people, and by the signs that it is allowed to work in the presence of the beast it deceives those who dwell on earth, telling them to make an image for the beast that was wounded by the sword and yet lived. And it was allowed to give breath to the image of the beast, so that the image of the beast might even speak and might cause those who would not worship the image of the beast to be slain. Also it causes all, both small and great, both rich and poor, both free and slave, to be marked on the right hand or the forehead, so that no one can buy or sell unless he has the mark, that is, the name of the beast or the number of its name. This calls for wisdom: let the one who has understanding calculate the number of the beast, for it is the number of a man, and his number is 666. (Rev 13:11–18)

The second beast is a false prophet (Rev 16:13; 19:20; 20:10). His signs are just like the ones used earlier by the two witnesses. The difference is that, while the two witnesses performed signs to lead people to faith in God, the false prophets wants to lead people astray and take them far from trusting God. The false prophet is just like his master, the devil, who is the father of lies. Jesus said it best: "The devil does not deal in the truth, because there is no truth in him. When he lies, he speaks out of his own character, for he is a liar and the father of lies" (John 8:44).

At this point, one might pause and wonder how this matters personally: "Who cares if the beast tries to deceive others? He won't deceive me. It is better to stay on the sidelines and not enter the battle." The problem with such sentiment is that the beast does not let us be neutral. He requires all people to wear his mark: 666. Much speculation has arisen over the number 666. Some people have claimed it is a computer chip, others suggest it is a mark similar to a barcode that allows personal information such as financial, academic, work, and medical histories to be accessed. In this view, instead of sending a resume, one simply gets scanned, and those unwilling to participate will effectively be shut out of society. Such speculation, though entertaining to contemplate, draws our attention away from the most important aspects of the mark.

First, there is a name associated with the number 666. The original readers of Revelation, would have known nothing about computer chips, barcodes, or laser scanners. When they heard the number 666, they would have thought about the wicked emperor Nero, whose full-name was Neron Caesar. This is important because in ancient numerology, letters bear numerical values. In Hebrew, the letters of Neron Caesar add up precisely to 666: *Nun* (50) + *Resh* (200) + *Waw* (6) + *Nun* (50) + *Qof* (100) + *Samech* (60) + *Resh* (200) = 666.[17]

נ	*Nun*	50
ר	*Resh*	200
ו	*Waw*	6
נ	*Nun*	50
ק	*Qof*	100
ס	*Samech*	60
ר	*Resh*	200
	TOTAL	666

Nero was the first Roman emperor to persecute the church. His persecution was so extensive that even after his death many

---

17. Boring, *Revelation*, 163.

believed he would rise from the grave and return to Asia Minor to further devastate Christians.[18]

Second, the mark functions as a sign of allegiance. People are either marked by the beast or marked by the Lamb. Either they will worship the dragon or worship the Creator. For those churches who struggle with assimilation (Ephesus, Pergamum, and Thyatira), as well as those who are complacent (Sardis and Laodicea), the temptation would be to simply accept the placement of the mark of the beast so as to not cause trouble. But to choose the Beast is to reject the Lamb.

Now we begin to understand the importance of military imagery. There is a battle between good and evil: God vs. Satan, the Lamb vs. the beast, the true witness vs. the false witness. It is a battle between life and death, between what is and what ought to be, between the way the world works and the way God works. And we find ourselves between these two warring sides.[19] *This is a war. One cannot remain neutral.*

> *O Church Arise and put your armor on*
> *Hear the call of Christ our Captain*
> *For now the weak can say that they are strong*
> *In the strength that God has given*
> *With shield of faith and belt of truth*
> *We'll stand against the devil's lies*
> *An army bold whose battle-cry is Love*
> *Reaching out to those in darkness*[20]

Thankfully, the old foe, the devil, has already received his mortal wound when Jesus rose from the grave. The devil still throws accusations at us, but we don't need to listen to them. The archangel Michael will not allow those accusations to come to God. And Jesus, who sits on the right hand of God, is our advocate.

---

18. Bauckham, *Climax of Prophecy*, 409.

19. Collins, *Crisis and Catharsis*, 141.

20. Keith Getty and Stuart Townend, "O Church Arise," *Thankyou Music* (Brentwood: Capital CMG, 2005), verse 1.

Refocus Questions

1. Do you like the "battle" metaphor used in these verses? What causes you to be nervous about the imagery? How might this metaphor provide comfort?

2. How important is it that Satan no longer has access to heaven and thus can no longer accuse you before God?

3. Part of the promise of a new eternity is a renewed creation (Rom 8). How important is it that we stand in solidarity with creation? In what ways might this encourage you to care for creation?

4. The first beast is a monster that causes people to wonder how they can endure. What are a few problems in this world that seem too big to engage?

5. Why do you think it is easy to worship the beast?

6. The beast works hard through smoke and mirrors to get false worship. Where do you see this happening in our world?

7. Why do you think endurance is so important in Christianity?

REVELATION 14–15

Whose Side Are You On?

Here is a call for the endurance of the saints, those who keep the commandments of God and their faith in Jesus. (Rev 14:12)

I WAS SEVEN THE first time I saw *Star Wars*. I was at a friend's house and he had a copy of the movie. I was amazed from start to finish. The special effects were tremendous and the story line was even better. I remember being terrified of Darth Vader. I was convinced there was no way the rebels could defeat the Death Star. And yet, I wanted to fight alongside Luke Skywalker, Han Solo, and Princess Leia. When the rebel fighters were victorious, I cheered and danced with the characters on the screen.

This success of the *Star Wars* movies is a bit fascinating, because the characters are not real and live in worlds unlike our own. And yet, these characters reveal deep connections to our own lives and human history. For instance, there was never a Darth Vader, but there has been an Adolf Hitler. There have never been Storm Troopers in space transports, but German SS troops acted as enforcers in Nazi Germany. The film's characters may be fictional, but their actions ring true, and that is what moves us.

The book of Revelation functions in a similar way. In the previous chapter we heard of a dragon. The last time I checked, while dragons exist in fantasy series on Netflix, there are no dragons flying around this world. But we can understand how a dragon personifies evil. Ask someone struggling with addiction if they are battling a dragon. Ask a person battling cancer. Ask someone with severe depression to describe their battle. It might sound very much like they are battling a dragon.

For the people of God, we battle forces that are as menacing as a dragon and as monstrous as the two beasts. We need a champion to fight for us. We need a rebellion to join. We need faith to endure.

THE REBELLION

Revelation 14 begins with the Lamb standing on Mount Zion. Clearly, the Lamb is our champion and he is standing on the high ground. The mention of Mount Zion is significant. Elisabeth Schüssler Fiorenza explains, "According to Isaiah 24:23; 25:7–10, at the end of time, God will be proclaimed king on Mount Zion, death will be destroyed, and God's people will be liberated from their oppression and the slander against them."[1] The prophet Joel also spoke salvation being given on Mount Zion to all who call on the name of the Lord (Joel 2:32). The Lamb has come to liberate his people.

Surrounding the Lamb are the 144,000. They are the same people mentioned in Rev 7:1–8. Remember, the 144,000 includes the great multitude that cannot be counted (see Rev 7:9).[2] This is important because standing with the Lord is his army of believers who oppose the followers of the beast. This is the rebellion.

> Then I looked, and behold, on Mount Zion stood the Lamb, and with him 144,000 who had his name and his Father's name written on their foreheads. And I heard a voice from heaven like the roar of many waters and like

1. Schüssler Fiorenza, *Revelation*, 87.
2. Collins, *Crisis and Catharsis*, 127.

the sound of loud thunder. The voice I heard was like the sound of harpists playing on their harps, and they were singing a new song before the throne and before the four living creatures and before the elders. No one could learn that song except the 144,000 who had been redeemed from the earth. It is these who have not defiled themselves with women, for they are virgins. It is these who follow the Lamb wherever he goes. These have been redeemed from mankind as firstfruits for God and the Lamb, and in their mouth no lie was found, for they are blameless. (Rev 14:1–5)

Three things stand out in this passage. First, the 144,000 are committed. They show their allegiance by having the name of the Lamb on their foreheads. In addition, they are virgins. This isn't a negative judgment on sex. It's simply a reference to the ancient practice of soldiers going into battle abstaining from sex (Deut 23:9–10). Later in Revelation, the notion of sexual infidelity will be connected to the violence, oppression, and greed fostered by Babylon the harlot (Rev 17:1–6; 18:3, 9). But here, the virgins are those who follow the Lamb and reject the practices associated with God's adversaries.[3] The 144,000 are committed and follow the Lamb wherever he goes, even into death (Rev 14:4b).[4]

Second, the 144,000 sing a new song. We are told that no one can learn the song except for the 144,000 (Rev 14:3). In truth, we have already heard this song in Rev 5:9–14.[5] Like all great protest songs, this is the song of rebellion by those who are determined to "Fight the Power."[6] One cannot truly learn the depths of this song's message unless one follows the Lamb.

---

3. Koester, *Revelation and the End of All Things*, 137.

4. Bauckham, *Climax of Prophecy*, 231.

5. Louis Brighton argues that "the new song" mentioned in Rev 14:3 is most likely identical to the "new song" mentioned in Rev 5:9. Brighton, *Revelation*, 369.

6. Public Enemy, "Fight the Power," on *Fear of a Black Planet* (Def Jam / Columbia, 1990).

Third, this army is the first fruits of the resurrection. In Jewish tradition, the first fruits were brought to the tabernacle as an offering before the rest of the harvest took place (Lev 23:10–14; Deut 26:1–11).[7] For this army, their sacrifice is the first fruits offering of a great harvest. This change of metaphor from military to farming is significant and tied together. Remember, this is a movement. It is about growth. One might say the seeds of rebellion have been sown and soon a harvest of revolt will occur. Unlike movements that seek to destroy, this movement seeks to liberate from those who destroy.

Speaking at an evangelism conference, Francis Chan told his audience about the importance of being committed to Christ and the harvest of faith: "I want us to really think through what we are trying to do, which is raise the dead, and it's not going to happen through our cleverness. It's going to happen by men and women being so attached to the vine that the fruits are just going to happen." Chan went on to say, "A movement starts when the founder really knows Jesus. You know how movements die? When the followers only know the founder [instead of Jesus]."[8] The 144,000 know the Lamb. They are dedicated. They know the song of redemption. They have learned this first hand. They are the first fruits of a great harvest.

A CALL TO ENDURE

The 144,000 know the Lamb. Do you? This question is so important that God sends three angels to preach the message of salvation to all the people of earth. Each message is a little different but, the goal is the same, namely, to create and sustain faith. The first angel speaks about the eternal gospel. The second angel declares that "Babylon has fallen." The third angel issues a warning about God's judgment.

> Then I saw *another angel* flying directly overhead, with an eternal gospel to proclaim to those who dwell on earth,

7. Koester, *Revelation*, 611.
8. Francis Chan, "Rethinking Outreach."

to every nation and tribe and language and people. And he said with a loud voice, "Fear God and give him glory, because the hour of his judgment has come, and worship him who made heaven and earth, the sea and the springs of water." *Another angel, a second,* followed, saying, "Fallen, fallen is Babylon the great, she who made all nations drink the wine of the passion of her sexual immorality." *And another angel, a third,* followed them, saying with a loud voice, "If anyone worships the beast and its image and receives a mark on his forehead or on his hand, he also will drink the wine of God's wrath, poured full strength into the cup of his anger, and he will be tormented with fire and sulfur in the presence of the holy angels and in the presence of the Lamb. And the smoke of their torment goes up forever and ever, and they have no rest, day or night, these worshipers of the beast and its image, and whoever receives the mark of its name." Here is a call for the endurance of the saints, those who keep the commandments of God and their faith in Jesus. And I heard a voice from heaven saying, "Write this: Blessed are the dead who die in the Lord from now on." "Blessed indeed," says the Spirit, "that they may rest from their labors, for their deeds follow them!" (Rev 14:6–13, italics mine)

The Greek word for "angel" means "messenger." These angels sent by God are preachers. The message is God's judgment. Most of us hear of God's judgment and think this is some bad news about eternal punishment. But God's judgment in this section is called "gospel" or "good news" (Rev 14:6).[9] The good news is that it is the enemies of God's people who will be judged and destroyed.

The second and third angels proclaim the destruction of Babylon and the enemies of God. The actual destruction of Babylon occurs later in Revelation 17 and 18. This announcement in ch. 14 serves as a warning: "If you take the mark of the beast, your end will be the same as Babylon." This is the judgment of God. This is also the good news for God's people who treasure the mark of the Lamb.

9. Boring, *Revelation,* 169.

As God's people, we are to engage in this battle. The dragon and beasts will attack. Many will die for the faith. But we must continue to fight and endure until God finishes the battle.

Louis Zamperini is one of the greatest examples of endurance. Zamperini endured a childhood of prejudice and poverty. He learned to run fast because he always ran from trouble. He became an Olympian and ran the 5000 meters in the 1936 Berlin Olympics. In 1940, Zamperini enlisted in the Army Air Corps. In 1943, his airplane crashed over the Pacific. He endured 47 days on the raft living off raw fish and rain water. He landed on a beach near the Philippines and was captured by Japanese soldiers. As such, he was tortured and abused by his captors. After being rescued, Zamperini had to face his hardest task of all: trying to live with the memory of his ordeal. At first, he could not endure. Understandably, Zamperini turned to alcohol to cope. But then he went to a Billy Graham meeting and, there, came to faith. It was through faith that Zamperini learned how to endure his awful past. It was through faith that he was able to forgive his captors. And now he rests in peace because he endured.[10]

> *O blessed saints, now take your rest;*
> *A thousand times shall you be blest*
> *For keeping faith*
> *From unto death*
> *And scorning worldly trust.*
> *For now you live at home with God*
> *And harvest seeds once cast abroad*
> *In tears and sighs.*
> *See with new eyes*
> *The pattern in the seed.*
> *The myriad angels raise their song.*
> *O saints, sing with that happy throng;*
> *Lift up one voice;*
> *Let heav'n rejoice*
> *In our redeemer's song!*[11]

10. See Hillenbrand, *Unbroken.*

11. Hans A. Brorson, "Behold the Hosts Arrayed in White," *Evangelical*

THE GRAPES OF WRATH

The warning to endure resounds throughout the remainder of the chapter as we are given a picture of the full wrath that God unleashes during this great judgment. As dire as the picture is, God's judgment is good news for the people of God because his wrath is directed at the enemies of God's people.

> Then I looked, and behold, a white cloud, and seated on the cloud one like a son of man, with a golden crown on his head, and a sharp sickle in his hand. And another angel came out of the temple, calling with a loud voice to him who sat on the cloud, "Put in your sickle, and reap, for the hour to reap has come, for the harvest of the earth is fully ripe." So he who sat on the cloud swung his sickle across the earth, and the earth was reaped. Then another angel came out of the temple in heaven, and he too had a sharp sickle. And another angel came out from the altar, the angel who has authority over the fire, and he called with a loud voice to the one who had the sharp sickle, "Put in your sickle and gather the clusters from the vine of the earth, for its grapes are ripe." So the angel swung his sickle across the earth and gathered the grape harvest of the earth and threw it into the great winepress of the wrath of God. And the winepress was trodden outside the city, and blood flowed from the winepress, as high as a horse's bridle, for 1,600 stadia. (Rev 14:14–20)

These words of judgment can be difficult to hear. The image of the Son of Man with a sickle harvesting the earth is intense. Furthermore, the idea of the enemies of God being thrown into a winepress (Rev 14:19) where they are crushed and their blood flows for 1,600 stadia (or 180 miles)[12] is gruesome. How do we make sense of such an image?

First, we must remember that it is Jesus who does the harvesting. He is not a grim reaper who cuts down indiscriminately.

Lutheran Worship (Minneapolis: Augsburg Fortress, 2006), 425, verse 3.

12. Schüssler Fiorenza, *Revelation*, 91.

Jesus has grace and mercy for the least, last, lost, and the little.[13] Jesus has grace and mercy for all who cry out for deliverance. It is those who oppose God's forgiveness that experience God's wrath.

Second, these words are meant to offer two alternatives: grain harvest or trampled grapes. Either we will be part of the great harvest of God (Rev 14:6–7) or we will be part of his wrath (Rev 14:19). It matters whose side we are on.

Finally, these words help God's people from seeking vengeance upon their enemies. It is easy to seek an eye for an eye. It is easy for people who are being persecuted to resort to violence and fulfill Steinbeck's words: "Someday—the armies of bitterness will all be going the same way . . . and there'll be a dread terror from it."[14] It would have been easy for Louis Zamperini to seek vengeance against his captors. But vengeance belongs to God and not us (Rom 12:29). Christ is the only one worthy to administer justice, and what we'll get from him is unexpected. Christ is the one who did not seek vengeance from those who killed him. Instead, he asked God the Father to forgive his captors. Will he do less for us?

A SONG FOR THE NATIONS

Revelation 15 shifts us back to heaven. We will discuss this vision in further detail in the next chapter. However, there is one important detail to examine, namely, the reference to the song of Moses (Rev 15:3). In the Old Testament, after God led the Israelites through the Red Sea and drowned Pharaoh's armies, Moses and the people sang a song praising God's victory over Egypt (Exod 15). It is natural for people to sing such songs. When a people has been oppressed, songs of violence are the natural inclination. In this passage, the song is not about victory over enemies, rather, it is a song about the conversion of the multitudes.

---

13. Capon, *Parables of the Kingdom*, 347.
14. Steinbeck, *Grapes of Wrath*, 111.

Then I saw another sign in heaven, great and amazing, seven angels with seven plagues, which are the last, for with them the wrath of God is finished. And I saw what appeared to be a sea of glass mingled with fire—and also those who had conquered the beast and its image and the number of its name, standing beside the sea of glass with harps of God in their hands. And they sing the song of Moses, the servant of God, and the song of the Lamb, saying, "Great and amazing are your deeds, O Lord God the Almighty! Just and true are your ways, O King of the nations! Who will not fear, O Lord, and glorify your name? For you alone are holy. All nations will come and worship you, for your righteous acts have been revealed." (Rev 15:1–4)

This song is important because it gets at the heart of God. God is interested in life, not destruction. This is the song of God's people. This is the song the 144,000 have learned. This is the song the church must sing. It matters whose side we are on. The beast uses fear and death to control the masses. The Lamb uses sacrifice. It appears the dragon and beasts have the upper hand, but it is the Lamb who stands on Mount Zion. It is the Lamb who is surrounded by the 144,000. It is the Lamb who judges the nations. It is the Lamb that allows all nations to worship God. Do you know the Lamb? Are you on his side? It matters because the Lamb alone is worthy of all worship and praise.

Refocus Questions

1. What is your favorite science-fiction movie? Why? How does it relate to everyday life?

2. The 144,000 are dedicated to God. What areas in your life reveal dedication to Christ?

3. The mention of God's judgment sounds like bad news but is really good news for God's people. What are some things in this world that you will be glad that God destroys?

4. The angels warn that Babylon will be destroyed. What warnings would angels deliver today?

5. Endurance is necessary as we wait for God's deliverance. What are some things that help you as you wait?

6. The grapes of wrath is a hard image for Christians. What comfort do you find in the fact that it is Jesus who judges the nations?

7. The people sang about the conversion of the nations, instead of the destruction of God's enemies. Why do you think this is important? Which is more likely to change hearts, the threat of destruction or the promise of grace in Christ?

CYCLE 5

SLAVERY

REVELATION 15–17

The Whore and the Bride

The waters that you saw, where the prostitute is seated, are peoples
and multitudes and nations and languages. And the ten horns that
you saw, they and the beast will hate the prostitute. They will make her
desolate and naked, and devour her flesh and burn her up with fire.

(Rev 17:15–16)

HISTORY IS FULL OF them. Some of their nicknames include:
Baghdad Bob, Tokyo Rose, Seoul City Sue, and Hanoi Hannah.
These are the nicknames of famous propagandists whose voices
were used to strengthen their own militaries while sowing seeds of
doubt among their enemies.

The Roman Empire had its share of propagandists. Although
we do not know many of their names, we know their message:
Rome is noble and invincible; bow to her. These propagandists
created and sustained their message by exalting the Roman Imperial Cult. By convincing people that the emperors were sons of the
gods and goddesses, they elevated Roman rulers to divine status
and so made the empire's conquest legitimate.

The propaganda worked. Many conquered peoples were defeated by this combination of Roman myth and might almost before any armies appeared. Even Christians were vulnerable to such propaganda. They struggled to distinguish the difference between Rome and their faith. Caesar Augustus had been hailed as the "Savior of the World." But Jesus was also confessed as the "Savior of the World." So, who was the real savior? Rome's clear and consistent message made it hard for Christians to distinguish the truth.

Things aren't so different in our time. There are many today who do not know how to separate their faith from their allegiance to their country, economic system, political affiliation, and the like. Christ has been used to justify capitalism, communism, and many other "isms." Loyalty to both God and country are almost a mantra for politicians. The idea of God's unity with a particular system or government is so entrenched in our psyches that it is hard to separate propaganda from the truth.

How does one fight such deception? One effective tool is satire. Through humor, ridicule, and parody, satirists help us see the absurdity of human behavior, vice, and folly. As Sophia Mc-Clennen explains, "Satire serves as a comedic and pedagogic form uniquely suited to provoking critical reflection." McClennen goes on to say, "Satire's ability to underscore the absurdity, ignorance, and prejudice of commonly accepted behavior by means of comedic critical reflection offers an especially potent form of public critique."[1] Think of Stephen Colbert. He can stand in the presence of world leaders and offer a scathing critique with a laugh. That is exactly what John does in chs. 15–17 of Revelation. John uses the image of the harlot to critique Rome.[2]

---

1. McClennen, *America according to Colbert*, 1.

2. Bauckham argues that "the book of Revelation is one of the fiercest attacks on Rome and one of the most effective pieces of political resistance literature from the period of the early empire." Bauckham, *Climax of Prophecy*, 338.

THE BOWLS OF WRATH

The fifth cycle begins where the previous cycle ends, with a triumphant song of praise rising from the assembly of the faithful.[3] Their song praises God, not for the destruction of their enemies, but for the conversion of the nations. This assembly has gathered around the "tent of witness" where the doors of the tent are open, allowing seven angels to process in and out. The "tent of witness" is a reference to the tabernacle (Exod 25:8–9), the portable worship space which the people of Israel used before the ark of the covenant was brought to Jerusalem by King David and a temple was built by his son, King Solomon. The tabernacle was a place for people on the move to encounter God who was also on the move in their lives. In this chapter, God is still on the move.

> After this I looked, and the sanctuary of the tent of witness in heaven was opened, and out of the sanctuary came the seven angels with the seven plagues, clothed in pure, bright linen, with golden sashes around their chests. And one of the four living creatures gave to the seven angels seven golden bowls full of the wrath of God who lives forever and ever, and the sanctuary was filled with smoke from the glory of God and from his power, and no one could enter the sanctuary until the seven plagues of the seven angels were finished. (Rev 15:5–8)

One of the four living creatures, previously mentioned in Revelation 4:6–7, gave a golden bowl to each of the seven angels. These are the same golden bowls that contained the prayers of the saints that were brought to God (Rev 5:8).[4] However, instead of prayers lifted up to God, these bowls contain God's wrath that will rain down upon those who worship the beast.

> Then I heard a loud voice from the temple telling the seven angels, "Go and pour out on the earth the seven bowls of the wrath of God." *So the first angel* went and

---

3. Koester, *Revelation and the End of All Things*, 145.
4. Schüssler Fiorenza, *Revelation*, 93.

poured out his bowl on the earth, and harmful and painful sores came upon the people who bore the mark of the
beast and worshiped its image. *The second angel* poured
out his bowl into the sea, and it became like the blood
of a corpse, and every living thing died that was in the
sea. *The third angel* poured out his bowl into the rivers
and the springs of water, and they became blood. And I
heard the angel in charge of the waters say, "Just are you,
O Holy One, who is and who was, for you brought these
judgments. For they have shed the blood of saints and
prophets, and you have given them blood to drink. It is
what they deserve!" And I heard the altar saying, "Yes,
Lord God the Almighty, true and just are your judgments!" *The fourth angel* poured out his bowl on the sun,
and it was allowed to scorch people with fire. They were
scorched by the fierce heat, and they cursed the name of
God who had power over these plagues. They did not
repent and give him glory. (Rev 16:1–9, italics mine)

The seven plagues follow a similar pattern as the seven trumpets did earlier (Rev 8–9). In parallel fashion, the first four trumpets and the first four bowls bring plagues upon the earth, sea,
land, and sun. The fifth trumpet and fifth bowl deal with the beast.
The sixth trumpet and sixth bowl deal with hostile armies that
gather near the Euphrates River.[5] Why the repeat? In one sense,
we have seen this throughout Revelation as a similar message is
spoken in different ways, just as individual verses in the Psalms
repeat their imagery. In another sense, the bowls of wrath address
a different audience than the trumpets. Where the seven trumpets
served to call God's people to bring God's promise to the lost, the
seven bowls of wrath call those who worship the beast to repent.

The horrors that are poured out of the bowls force us to face
the question of whether God's wrath is compatible with God's love.
To say it another way, how can a loving God act wrathfully and
bring these things into people's lives? Looking at how God's wrath
functions in this section can help us understand this.

---

5. Koester, *Revelation and the End of All Things*, 148.

The first bowl of wrath, gives painful sores on the skin of those who wear the mark of the beast [see 13:16]. The second and third bowls turn the sea and water ways into blood, forcing those who shed the blood of the saints to drink blood. The fourth bowl is poured upon the sun, causing severe heat to harm the followers of the beast. As the bowls are poured out, the angel says God's wrath is just. (Rev 16:5–6)

Seeing this as just can be a foreign idea for us and even seems like an argument for not trusting God. Earlier, in Revelation 6:9–11, the saints under the altar cried "how long" as they waited for God's justice. The saints were killed by God's enemies because of their faithfulness to the gospel. Their enemies only have to drink blood (Rev 16:6). This justice does not seem strong enough. But the saints know that God's justice is never solely about retribution. God's justice is always about making things right and is ever mixed with grace and mercy. They know this because it is on the cross where God's mercy and justice meet. As the psalmist says, "Steadfast love and faithfulness will meet; righteousness and peace will kiss each other" (Ps 85: 10). God's own being is where mercy and justice come together. We can't have one without the other. This is why those at the altar (including the saints under the altar) say, "Yes, Lord God the Almighty, true and just are your judgments!" (Rev 16:7). Like the work of a gardener who both weeds and fertilizes in order to produce a bountiful harvest, God's wrath is both loving and just because God's purpose is to create and sustain life. This is much like the way parents will correct their children so that they will not play in the street. Sometimes saying "No!" is the most loving thing a person can say.

What does this mean for today? I'm reminded of Winston who was a fixture at my home church. Winston knew the Bible better than most people, but he never preached or taught others. He would do the hardest of tasks behind the scenes but never anything in front. One day, I asked him why he only worked behind the scenes. To explain, he told me his story.

Winston grew up in a brothel, became a pimp, and had killed a man. He, went to jail and served his sentence. While in jail, Winston came to faith in Christ. He began reading his Bible. When he was released from jail, he volunteered at church. He always served in lowly positions because he believed that was his penance for his previous life. According to justice, Winston took a life and thus his life should be taken from him. However, he received a justice filled with mercy. He no longer worshiped the beast. He worshiped the Lamb. Winston is a living witness of John Wesley's powerful hymn, "And Can It Be."

> And can it be that I should gain
> an interest in the Savior's blood!
> Died he for me? who caused his pain!
> For me? who him to death pursued?
> Amazing love! How can it be
> that thou, my God, shouldst die for me?
> Amazing love! How can it be
> that thou, my God, shouldst die for me?[6]

Winston repented. Unfortunately, those who followed the beast refused to repent. If they had, the bowls of wrath would no longer be necessary. But those beast-followers refused to repent! As a result, the chapter continues as the fifth and sixth bowls are poured out.

> *The fifth angel* poured out his bowl on the throne of the beast, and its kingdom was plunged into darkness. People gnawed their tongues in anguish and cursed the God of heaven for their pain and sores. They did not repent of their deeds. *The sixth angel* poured out his bowl on the great river Euphrates, and its water was dried up, to prepare the way for the kings from the east. (Rev 16:1–12, italics mine)

No longer is God's wrath simply directed toward the followers of the beast. These bowls are directed at the beast itself. The

6. Charles Wesley, "And Can It Be, That I Should Gain," *The United Methodist Hymnal* (Nashville: Abingdon, 1989), 363, verse 1.

fifth bowl is poured on the throne of the beast leading to a plague of darkness. Remember that the dragon gave the throne to the beast (Rev 13:2, 5–8) which led to the beast "blaspheming God, slaughtering the saints, and demanding allegiance from people of every tribe and nation."[7] God's wrath is poured out on the beast's throne.

The sixth bowl is poured on the Euphrates, causing the water to dry up. With the river dried up, the beast's army is vulnerable to attack from the east. This is the very threat mentioned from the first of the four riders who arrived on its horse with a bow (Rev 6:2). Beware, if one serves in the beast's army, he or she is exposed. Repent and worship God.

ARMAGEDDON

Knowing they are vulnerable, the dragon and two beasts send forth a warning. They release frogs (unclean animals) from their mouths to rally the kings of this world for a great battle at a place called Armageddon.

> And I saw, coming out of the mouth of the dragon and out of the mouth of the beast and out of the mouth of the false prophet, three unclean spirits like frogs. For they are demonic spirits, performing signs, who go abroad to the kings of the whole world, to assemble them for battle on the great day of God the Almighty. ("Behold, I am coming like a thief! Blessed is the one who stays awake, keeping his garments on, that he may not go about naked and be seen exposed!") And they assembled them at the place that in Hebrew is called Armageddon. (Rev 16:13–16)

The name "Armageddon" has captured the imagination of many, often with irrational ideas. Armageddon is the place where a final battle is supposed to happen between God's army and that of the beast. Much ink has been expended in speculating the exact

---

7. Koester, *Revelation and the End of All Things*, 151.

location of this future battlefield. The only problem is that no such place exists. In Hebrew, Armageddon is a combination of two names: Har (Mountain) and Megiddo (a plain in Northern Israel). Thus, Armageddon is the mountain at Megiddo. The only problem is that there are no mountains at Megiddo. The nearest mountain is Mount Carmel,[8] the place where Elijah called down fire to defeat Queen Jezebel's prophets (1 Kgs 18).

The reference to a mountain at Megiddo is a symbol. Megiddo was an important location in Israel's history. In Judges 5:10, the female judge Deborah led Israel's armies in a decisive victory at Megiddo. Later, King Josiah was killed at Megiddo because he didn't listen to God (2 Chr 33:20–24). We could might say that Megiddo is a place where the enemies of God meet their end. Combine that with the idea of a mountain (remember in the Bible there are many famous mountains where God acts: Ararat, Sinai, Horeb, Carmel, Zion, etc.) and we can begin to understand what is happening. Armageddon is used here not as the designation of a particular geographical location, but as a terrifying metaphor and warning for those who will not repent.[9]

Before the battle can occur, the seventh angel throws his bowl into the air releasing the final wrath of God.

> The seventh angel poured out his bowl into the air, and a loud voice came out of the temple, from the throne, saying, "It is done!" And there were flashes of lightning, rumblings, peals of thunder, and a great earthquake such as there had never been since man was on the earth, so great was that earthquake. The great city was split into three parts, and the cities of the nations fell, and God remembered Babylon the great, to make her drain the cup of the wine of the fury of his wrath. And every island fled away, and no mountains were to be found. And great hailstones, about one hundred pounds each, fell from heaven on people; and they cursed God for the plague of the hail, because the plague was so severe. (Rev 16:17–21)

8. Caird, *Revelation of St. John*, 207.

9. Brighton, *Revelation*, 423.

A voice cries out from the throne, "It is done!" Accompanying these words are acts of nature so tremendous that only God could orchestrate them. This is theophany as God is revealed and judgment is directed at Babylon who is forced to drink the entire cup of God's wrath (Rev 16:19). Earlier, the whore (Babylon) made the wicked drink from her cup. Now she must drink every last drop.

What is most striking is not the "act of God," but rather the unwillingness of people to repent. Unlike Winston at my home congregation, who walked the long road of repentance, followers of the beast refuse to leave the evil in which they are enmeshed. They are addicted to the beast and its allure of power and pleasure. They have tasted evil and simply want more of it no matter the cost. But John's vision announces that they must repent or be destroyed. People cannot stand counter to God and prevail. In love, God lessens his wrath to provide time for repentance.

> The Lord is not slow to fulfill his promise as some count slowness, but is patient toward you, not wishing that any should perish, but that all should reach repentance. (2 Pet 3:9)

THE GREAT WHORE

Once again the scene shifts. This time, one of the seven angels carries us to the wilderness where we find the Great Whore (see fig. 8). The last time John's vision took us to the wilderness we saw the virtuous woman escape from the dragon (Rev 12). This time, it is the other woman, the whore, who is sitting on the beast.

> Then one of the seven angels who had the seven bowls came and said to me, "Come, I will show you the judgment of the great prostitute who is seated on many waters, with whom the kings of the earth have committed sexual immorality, and with the wine of whose sexual immorality the dwellers on earth have become drunk." And he carried me away in the Spirit into a wilderness, and I saw a woman sitting on a scarlet beast that was full of blasphemous

The Whore of Babylon by Albrecht Dürer

XV

Description (Figure 8): In lower right is the harlot on the
beast. You can see the seventh head is turned toward her,
ready to attack. Behind her is the fire that will consume
her remains. In the upper left corner is the rider on the
white horse (Rev 19) who will soon come to fight.

names, and it had seven heads and ten horns. The woman was arrayed in purple and scarlet, and adorned with gold and jewels and pearls, holding in her hand a golden cup full of abominations and the impurities of her sexual immorality. And on her forehead was written a name of mystery: "Babylon the great, mother of prostitutes and of earth's abominations." And I saw the woman, drunk with the blood of the saints, the blood of the martyrs of Jesus. When I saw her, I marveled greatly. (Rev 17:1–6)

With these words, John paints a vivid picture of the harlot. The harlot sits on a beast with seven heads and holds a goblet filled with the blood of the saints. To understand this image, one needs to look at a Roman coin with the goddess Roma on it. The coin is how Rome wanted to portray itself.

How Rome saw itself	How John saw Rome
Woman sits on a throne of 7 hills	Sits on beast with 7 heads
Noble and virtuous	Drunken Whore
Sitting with a sword in hand	Holding a goblet full of blood

The contrast is significant. Rome's propaganda manipulated people to see the goddess Roma sitting calmly on a throne of seven hills which highlight Rome's seven hills. Roma is portrayed as a noble and virtuous woman who holds a sword as a reminder of the *Pax Romana* (Roman Peace). John contrasts the common understanding of this symbol of the empire by depicting Roma as a drunken whore who sits on a seven-headed beast. She is drunk on the blood of the saints. This is satire! Rome's "justice" is exposed as power for Roman nobles and nobody else. There is no justice to be found in the world's powers, but it can be found in God.

No one knows the power of satire more than the people who work for the magazine *Charlie Hebdo*. The satire magazine is famous, and infamous, for skewering nearly everything, especially sacred cows. But standing up against power through satire has been costly. On January 7, 2015, masked terrorists killed twelve people in an assault on the magazine's Paris offices because of satirical cartoons they published about the Muslim prophet Muhammad.[10]

The introduction to this apocalypse tells us that John was exiled and imprisoned on the island Patmos "because of the word of God and the testimony of Jesus (Rev 1:9)." The powerful do not like those who critique them or question their power. Even though John criticizes Rome specifically, his words can be applied to any emperor, king, general, president, dictator, movement, etc. Satire has a way of taking power away from those who attempt to manipulate others.

THE WHORE'S DEMISE

Rome is a harlot. Rome is not virtuous. Rome uses and abuses people. But why not just go along with the lie and accommodate Rome's power? Why not simply benefit by being joined with the harlot? The answer is clear: There's no future in it, because the whore dies.

> But the angel said to me, "Why do you marvel? I will tell you the mystery of the woman, and of the beast with seven heads and ten horns that carries her. The beast that you saw was, and is not, and is about to rise from the bottomless pit and go to destruction. And the dwellers on earth whose names have not been written in the book of life from the foundation of the world will marvel to see the beast, because it was and is not and is to come.

10. Wilkinson, "Satire and Terrorism."

This calls for a mind with wisdom: the seven heads are seven mountains on which the woman is seated; they are also seven kings, five of whom have fallen, one is, the other has not yet come, and when he does come he must remain only a little while. As for the beast that was and is not, it is an eighth but it belongs to the seven, and it goes to destruction. And the ten horns that you saw are ten kings who have not yet received royal power, but they are to receive authority as kings for one hour, together with the beast. These are of one mind, and they hand over their power and authority to the beast. They will make war on the Lamb, and the Lamb will conquer them, for he is Lord of lords and King of kings, and those with him are called and chosen and faithful." And the angel said to me, "The waters that you saw, where the prostitute is seated, are peoples and multitudes and nations and languages. And the ten horns that you saw, they and the beast will hate the prostitute. They will make her desolate and naked, and devour her flesh and burn her up with fire, for God has put it into their hearts to carry out his purpose by being of one mind and handing over their royal power to the beast, until the words of God are fulfilled. And the woman that you saw is the great city that has dominion over the kings of the earth." (Rev 17:7–18)

It is no surprise that God wins against his enemies. It's where things have been heading all along. However, it is the method by which the whore dies that is surprising. The whore is eaten by the beast she rides (Rev 17:16)! The nature of evil is self-destruction. The beast and its allies begin by waging war against the lamb, but the beast turns on the harlot and eats her. She who consumed the blood of the saints is now consumed by the beast and her remains are burned with fire. She's not so powerful now.

That is the point. That is the satire. The woman on the beast might appear to be lovely and noble, but she isn't. She is a drunken prostitute. She will not prevail. She will be destroyed. Evil always loses. God's justice will prevail. If you follow the beast, repent! The Roman Empire and its ruler may no longer exist, but other powers rise in every age, and the beast is still active today. Even in America, there are forces that promise delight but, in the end, consume and destroy. What are the things today that rob freedom? What are the things that consume?

Refocus Questions

1. Can a loving God be wrathful? Why or why not?

2. The first four bowls of wrath are directed at those who worship the beast. Do you like the idea that God's justice toward them is not retribution (an eye for an eye) but rather justice mixed with mercy? Why or why not?

3. Megiddo is the place where the enemies of God are destroyed. Do you like this symbol?

4. Rome saw itself as a noble woman whereas John saw Rome as a drunken harlot. Are there things in this world that are idolized when in truth they should be condemned?

5. Do you like John's use of satire? Why do you think satire is such a strong weapon? What picture might John use for governments, politicians, leaders, and celebrities to whom we look today?

6. The harlot is destroyed by the beast; in other words, evil destroys itself. Why is this a comforting message?

7. What is the beast for you? Clearly, it is no longer Rome, but the beast is still active today. What are the things that rob you of your freedom? What are the things that consume you?

REVELATION 18–19

Whom Do You Love?

Come out of her, my people, lest you take part in her sins, lest you share
in her plagues; for her sins are heaped high as heaven, and God has
remembered her iniquities. (Rev 18:4–5)

IT SEEMS RIGGED! WALL Street, the banks, and world governments
each have the power to alter billions of lives. A nation goes to war,
and millions of refugees flee their homes. Banks manipulate sub-
prime rates, and the housing market is destroyed. CEOs appease
their investors, and jobs are sent overseas. In each case, those in
power use their position for selfish gain with dire consequences for
the most vulnerable. In his book *Saving Capitalism for the Many
Not the Few*, former Labor Secretary Robert Reich addresses the
growing income gap between the rich and poor. Reich explains,
"In the 1950s and '60s, CEOs of large corporations earned an aver-
age of about twenty times the pay of their typical worker. Now
they get substantially over two hundred times."[1] During the
Roman Empire, wealth was also concentrated among the elite

1. Reich, *Saving Capitalism*, xi.

who exploited their subjects. The entire Roman economic system manipulated and marginalized the masses. When John calls Rome both harlot and Babylon, he does so because "Rome resembled the Old Testament Babylon in being a proud, idolatrous, oppressive empire that used power to conquer and oppress the people of God."[2] To side with Rome was to side with the people in power who subjugated the nations.

How are Christians to move forward when forces are beyond their control? Is the answer to simply accept the order of things? Is the answer to fight? Are we to occupy Wall Street or join the Tea Party? Are labor unions the answer or should we deregulate the markets? Revelation 18 and 19 know nothing about our economic system and can't possibly answer these questions directly. But they do challenge the alliances and concessions Christians make to those in power.

WHY WAS THE WHORE DESTROYED?

Revelation 18 begins with a scene similar to the zombie movie *I Am Legend* (2007). The movie begins with a city void of life but filled with zombies. Like the movie, the streets of Babylon are empty except for the foul creatures that inhabit it. Babylon, the city that once attracted the most prestigious people, now is a place for demons and scavenging birds. After the whore's demise (Rev 17:16–18), an angel arrives from heaven with immense authority and explains why Babylon, the great whore, was destroyed.

> After this I saw another angel coming down from heaven, having great authority, and the earth was made bright with his glory. And he called out with a mighty voice, "Fallen, fallen is Babylon the great! She has become a dwelling place for demons, a haunt for every unclean spirit, a haunt for every unclean bird, a haunt for every unclean and detestable beast. For all nations have drunk the wine of the passion of her sexual immorality, and the

2. Bauckham, *Climax of Prophecy*, 345.

kings of the earth have committed immorality with her,
and the merchants of the earth have grown rich from the
power of her luxurious living." (Rev 18:1–3)

Babylon is called a whore because those who associate with
a harlot must pay for the privilege of intimacy with her. Rome was
no ordinary whore; she was a rich courtesan. Her expensive clothes
and jewelry (Rev 17:4) reveal the luxurious lifestyle she maintains
at her lovers' expense and belie the emptiness at her core.[3] The
harlot becomes rich on the allure of relationship, but in truth simply lives a lie. As Eugene Peterson explains, "The truth of life is
that love is a gift. . . . The whore's lie is that love is purchased, that
relationships are 'deals' and sexuality is an appetite. Whoredom is
the use of good to do evil."[4] All of life becomes a transaction, and
people become commodities to be traded or marketed to. Babylon
is a picture of sin. As Martin Luther argues, "Sin is being so deeply
curved in on itself that it bends the best gifts of God towards itself
and enjoys them."[5] The harlot is destroyed, because she has taken
wealth and used it for herself and not for others. The great irony is
that the one who made others die of consumption is now the one
consumed.

It is no surprise that the nations are seduced by the harlot.
Power is seductive and sings a siren song. The surprise occurs
in the following verses as we learn Christians also have intimate
knowledge of the whore.

> Then I heard another voice from heaven saying, "Come
> out of her, my people, lest you take part in her sins, lest
> you share in her plagues; for her sins are heaped high
> as heaven, and God has remembered her iniquities. Pay
> her back as she herself has paid back others, and repay
> her double for her deeds; mix a double portion for her
> in the cup she mixed. As she glorified herself and lived
> in luxury, so give her a like measure of torment and

3. Ibid., 347.
4. Peterson, *Reverse Thunder*, 147.
5. Luther, *Lectures on Romans*, 345.

mourning, since in her heart she says, 'I sit as a queen, I am no widow, and mourning I shall never see.' For this reason her plagues will come in a single day, death and mourning and famine, and she will be burned up with fire; for mighty is the Lord God who has judged her." (Rev 18:4–8)

"Come out of her, my people . . ." (Rev 18:4). Christians are people who have come to trust that all good gifts come from God. Christians also believe that God blesses us that we might become a blessing to others (Gen 12:1–3). In this passage John exposes the terrible truth that Christians often worship the harlot instead of their creator.

Joey was a man in need of a place to stay. He was a Christian but was also an addict. His addiction to drugs and fast money destroyed his marriage and nearly destroyed his life. Joey pulled into the church parking lot with a camper and asked if he could park it there for a few days. When those days passed, he asked to stay longer and began working at the church as a janitor. The church allowed him to do the custodial work on the condition that he attend our weekly Alcoholics Anonymous group and weekly Bible study. Over time, he started attending more community Bible studies and continued to work on his sobriety. A decade later, Joey is now a pastor in a Southern California church with a thriving ministry. Joey knew what it was like to be lured in by the harlot. Thankfully, he heard Christ's call to come out of her. Whether the issue is wealth, power, addiction, pornography, or anything else, it is easy to be seduced by the harlot. It is costly to know the whore. Listen to Christ's call, "Come out of her my people!"

THE WHORE'S FUNERAL

In the remainder of Revelation 18, we attend the whore's funeral. At this funeral are three sets of mourners. The first group are the rulers of the earth. These rulers are the very ones who received their authority from Rome.[6] They mourn because in cozying up to her, they commit illicit acts with her and will meet the same fate:

> And the kings of the earth, who committed sexual immorality and lived in luxury with her, will weep and wail over her when they see the smoke of her burning. They will stand far off, in fear of her torment, and say, "Alas! Alas! You great city, you mighty city, Babylon! For in a single hour your judgment has come" (Rev 18:9–10).

The second group of mourners are the merchants who made significant money by trading with the harlot. These merchants mourn because "no one buys their cargo anymore" (Rev 18:11). Listen to the items that were traded:

> And the merchants of the earth weep and mourn for her, since no one buys their cargo anymore, cargo of gold, silver, jewels, pearls, fine linen, purple cloth, silk, scarlet cloth, all kinds of scented wood, all kinds of articles of ivory, all kinds of articles of costly wood, bronze, iron and marble, cinnamon, spice, incense, myrrh, frankincense, wine, oil, fine flour, wheat, cattle and sheep, horses and chariots, and slaves, that is, human souls. "The fruit for which your soul longed has gone from you, and all your delicacies and your splendors are lost to you, never to be found again!" (Rev 18:11–14)

This list is significant because it shows the reach of Rome's economy. Rome imported gold and silver from Spain, precious jewels from India, pearls from the Red Sea. Fine linens arrived from Egypt. Silk came from China. Scarlet from Asia Minor. Citrus wood from Morocco. Ivory came from North Africa and India. Costly wood from Africa and India. Iron from Spain and Pontus. Marble from Africa, Egypt, and Greece. Cinnamon was imported from south Asia. Incense from the East and wine from Sicily and Spain.[7] This was a world economy and Rome was the primary

---

6. Bauckham, *Climax of Prophecy*, 372.

7. Ibid., 350–66.

beneficiary. As Richard Bauckham explains, "The Pax Romana was really a system of economic exploitation of the empire. Rome's subjects gave far more to her than she gave to them."[8] It is costly to have intimate knowledge of the whore.

The final group of mourners are the mariners who transported the goods. In AD 155, Aelius Aristides delivered these words before the imperial court in Rome: "So many merchants' ships arrive here, conveying every kind of goods from every people every hour and every day, so that the city is like a factory common to the whole earth." Aristides goes on to say, "The arrivals and departures of the ships never stop. . . . Whatever one does not see here, is not a thing which has existed or exists."[9] This description sounds a lot like the Port of Los Angeles today where cargo ships line up to deliver goods. These mariners weep over lost profits because they "grew rich by her wealth" (Rev 18:19).

> The merchants of these wares, who gained wealth from her, will stand far off, in fear of her torment, weeping and mourning aloud, "Alas, alas, for the great city that was clothed in fine linen, in purple and scarlet, adorned with gold, with jewels, and with pearls! For in a single hour all this wealth has been laid waste." And all shipmasters and seafaring men, sailors and all whose trade is on the sea, stood far off and cried out as they saw the smoke of her burning, "What city was like the great city?" And they threw dust on their heads as they wept and mourned, crying out, "Alas, alas, for the great city where all who had ships at sea grew rich by her wealth! For in a single hour she has been laid waste. Rejoice over her, O heaven, and you saints and apostles and prophets, for God has given judgment for you against her!" (Rev 18:15–20)

Looking at this list of mourners, there is one group that does not cry at the harlot's death, namely, the "human souls" or slaves that Rome traded (Rev 18:14). Enslaved people were Rome's most important commodity because, as in the southern states of

8. Ibid., 347.
9. Ibid., 376.

America before the Civil War, slavery propped up the entire economy. Without enslaved labor, there could be no luxury. Rome was neither the first nor the last country to enslave people and trade them as a commodity. Historian Adam Hochschild tells how prevalent enslavement has been in human cultures: "Slaves were spread throughout the Islamic world, and the Ottoman Empire. . . . In India and other parts of Asia, tens of millions of farmworkers were slaves. Native Americans turned prisoners of war into slaves and sold them to other tribes. . . . In Russia the majority of the population were serfs, often bought, sold, whipped, or sent to the army at the will of their owners." In fact, by the end of the eighteenth century "well over three-quarters of all people alive in the world were either slaves or serfs."[10]

One famous slave trader was John Newton. At the age of eighteen, Newton was kidnapped by the British Navy and pressed into service on the HMS *Harwich*. Over the next year, he was chained, flogged, and shot at in battle. Upon his release, he worked in the buying and selling of enslaved people. Newton gladly joined this trade because it meant both release from the navy as well as a path to wealth and respectability in society. Of course, there was nothing respectable about the slave trade. Newton, along with the other sailors, abused the slaves and raped the female captives. Each day on the ship, Newton found himself in a more and more wretched state.

One day, a violent storm thrashed against the ship. In despair, Newton cried out to the Lord. The storm ceased as it did for the disciples in the boat when Jesus calmed the winds and the waves, and Newton was changed. Newton didn't immediately cease his involvement in enslaving others. He worked in the trade for another decade. However, something began to slowly change in him. He began to attend worship and to pray. He was married, and he began to be more humane in his treatment of those whose freedom he controlled. It was not until 1788, thirty-four years after leaving the slave trade, that he publicly renounced his former profession

10. Hochschild, *Bury the Chains*, 2.

and published a pamphlet titled "Thoughts upon the Slave Trade." The tract described the horrific conditions on slave ships. The pamphlet was so popular it was reprinted numerous times and sent to every member of Parliament. Under the leadership of William Wilberforce, the English civil government outlawed slavery in Great Britain in 1807. As influential as the pamphlet was, Newton is most remembered for writing the hymn "Amazing Grace":[11]

> Amazing Grace, how sweet the sound,
> That saved a wretch like me.
> I once was lost but now am found,
> Was blind, but now I see.[12]

It took Newton thirty-four years before he could see the evil of enslaving others. Thankfully, God is not blind to this world's bondage. When God's chosen people were in Egypt, God delivered them with an outstretched hand. When we were in bondage to sin, God delivered us by sending Jesus. At the heart of God's being is freedom. As Paul writes to the people of Galatia, "For freedom Christ has set us free; stand firm therefore, and do not submit again to a yoke of slavery" (Gal 5:1). The whore is destroyed because she enslaves.

Revelation 18 ends the way it began, namely, with an angel proclaiming the complete devastation of Babylon. The lights have been turned out on the wicked city. The party is over. The music has stopped. And the piper must be paid.

> Then a mighty angel took up a stone like a great millstone and threw it into the sea, saying, "So will Babylon the great city be thrown down with violence, and will be found no more; and the sound of harpists and musicians, of flute players and trumpeters, will be heard in you no more, and a craftsman of any craft will be found in you no more, and the sound of the mill will be heard in you no more, and the light of a lamp will shine in you

11. Ibid., 11–29, 75–77, 131–32.

12. John Newton, "Amazing Grace," *Evangelical Lutheran Worship* (Minneapolis: Augsburg Fortress, 2006), 779, verse 1.

no more, and the voice of bridegroom and bride will be heard in you no more, for your merchants were the great ones of the earth, and all nations were deceived by your sorcery. And in her was found the blood of prophets and of saints, and of all who have been slain on earth." (Rev 18:20–24)

It is costly to sidle up next to the whore. Her fate is sealed, but ours is not, for God says, "Come out of her my people!"

HALLELUJAH!

In Revelation 19, the scene radically shifts from earth to heaven, from a funeral to a celebration. Instead, of tears, there are shouts of joy. The harlot is dead. God's people prevail. No other word is more appropriate for such a moment as the Hebrew word *hallelujah!* which means "praise" (*hallel*) "the Lord" (*Jah*—a shortened version of *Yahweh*, one of God's names in the Old Testament). Four times the word hallelujah is shouted:

> After this I heard what seemed to be the loud voice of a great multitude in heaven, crying out, "Hallelujah! Salvation and glory and power belong to our God, for his judgments are true and just; for he has judged the great prostitute who corrupted the earth with her immorality, and has avenged on her the blood of his servants." Once more they cried out, "Hallelujah! The smoke from her goes up forever and ever." And the twenty-four elders and the four living creatures fell down and worshiped God who was seated on the throne, saying, "Amen. Hallelujah!" And from the throne came a voice saying, "Praise our God, all you his servants, you who fear him, small and great." Then I heard what seemed to be the voice of a great multitude, like the roar of many waters and like the sound of mighty peals of thunder, crying out, "Hallelujah! For the Lord our God the Almighty reigns." (Rev 19:1–6)

The first hallelujah (Rev 19:1) celebrates the truth and righteousness of God's judgment. The second hallelujah (Rev 19:3) is shouted in gratitude that the harlot's smoke ascends forever. In other words, she has been completely destroyed. The third hallelujah (Rev 19:4) circles back to the beginning of Revelation and is spoken by the twenty-four elders and four creatures as they call on the whole community to cry a loud hallelujah. This is significant because Babylon treated the lowly as property whereas, in the heavenly vision, both the great and small have a place in the congregation. The final hallelujah (Rev 19:6) is the congregation's response to all that God has done.[13]

When the ex-addict Joey told me that he wanted to be a pastor, I feared for him because I did not know if the pressures of ministry would be too much for him. However, I was proven wrong. Seeing him preach was one of the greatest moments of my life. There were no words that could sum up my joy over God's victory over what bound him except, "Praise the Lord!" (hallelujah).

> *Hallelujah Hallelujah Hallelujah Hallelujah Hallelujah*
> *For the Lord God omnipotent reigneth*
> *Hallelujah Hallelujah Hallelujah Hallelujah.*[14]

With all this celebration, it becomes apparent that something more fun than a funeral is going to take place. A wedding is about to occur between the Lamb and the Bride. The wedding stands in contrast to the funeral, just as the bride stands in contrast to the whore.

> "Let us rejoice and exult and give him the glory, for the marriage of the Lamb has come, and his Bride has made herself ready; it was granted her to clothe herself with fine linen, bright and pure"—for the fine linen is the righteous deeds of the saints. And the angel said to me, "Write this: Blessed are those who are invited to the marriage supper of the Lamb." And he said to me, "These are the true words of God." Then I fell down at his feet to worship him, but he said to me, "You must not do that! I

---

13. Peterson, *Reversed Thunder*, 149–50.

14. George F. Handel, "Hallelujah Chorus," *Messiah*, Novello ed. (London: Novello, 1959).

am a fellow servant with you and your brothers who hold
to the testimony of Jesus. Worship God." For the testimony of Jesus is the spirit of prophecy. (Rev 19:7–10)

Everything about the bride is different from the harlot. The
harlot was clothed in scarlet fabric that declares her body for sale,
(Rev 18:16) but the bride wears linen made from the "righteous
deeds of the saints." The harlot has sex for money, but the bride
marries for love. As Eugene Peterson explains, "For the Whore,
sex is a service of commerce; for the Bride, sex is devoted to love.
For the Whore, sex is a contract; for the Bride, sex is a life com-
mitment. For the Whore, sex is a calculation; for the Bride, sex is
an offering."[15] The bride loves the Lamb because he has purchased
her freedom through his death and resurrection.

> *The church's one foundation is Jesus Christ, her Lord;*
> *she is his new creation by water and the Word.*
> *From heaven he came and sought her to be his holy bride;*
> *with his own blood he bought her, and for her life he*
> *died.*[16]

The point is simple: do not unite yourself with the whore. Intimacy with her will cost everything. Instead, worship God and the
Lamb. It matters whom we worship. Too many of us are blinded
by corrupt activities and power-mongering in this world. In many
ways, we are blind like John Newton was to the exploitation of
the poor. We do not own slaves, but like the Israelites whom God
sent the Old Testament prophets to condemn, we pursue riches on
the back of the most vulnerable. We did not, of course, create this
arrangement, but we also do nothing to stop it. We have joined the
harlot and her economics. We need to hear the words of our Lord
as he says, "Come out of her my people!"

---

15. Peterson, *Reversed Thunder*, 147.

16. Samuel Stone, "The Church's One Foundation," *Evangelical Lutheran
Worship* (Minneapolis: Augsburg Fortress, 2006), 654, verse 1.

Refocus Questions

1. If John wrote about America today, how might he critique our current economic system?

2. Who are the rulers today who have received power from the whore?

3. Who are the merchants today who make money off the whore?

4. How are people today being enslaved, traded, and exploited? What enslaves you?

5. Why do you think freedom is so important to God?

6. How can the church be an agent of change in our society? What are things you can do?

7. What is God calling you to come out of today?

CYCLE 6

NEWNESS

REVELATION 19–20

God Is Making All Things New

Then I saw heaven opened, and behold, a white horse! The one sitting
on it is called Faithful and True, and in righteousness he judges and
makes war. (Rev 19:11)

ONE OF THE HARDEST things I had to experience was the death
of my mother-in-law. Not everyone is as blessed as I was to have
such an amazing in-law. Vicki was a beautiful woman. She was
a good mother, a gracious wife, and a faithful Christian. In fact,
she prayed for her daughter's future husband (me) throughout my
wife's childhood.

Our family was devastated when Vicki was diagnosed with
cancer. The oncologist told her she had less than a year to live.
Vicki fought, prayed, lived, loved, and struggled for two years beyond that initial year. Anyone who has lost a loved one to cancer
knows the cruelty of the illness.

The last time I saw Vicki in this life, I prayed with her, read her
scripture, and told her how thankful I was for her love. I promised
that I would take care of her daughter and granddaughters. Then it
was time to say goodbye. As I got up to leave, she grabbed my arm

and said, "The rider's name is 'Faithful and True'" (Rev 19:11). This part of John's vision is where Vicki's words to me are found.

Living in this world is not easy. Looking around, it can seem like the dragon is winning. People struggle with illness and depression, loss and addiction, hunger and despair, warfare, strife, and famine. Even if we somehow miss these struggles, death comes for us all. As Brian Blount explains, "The dragon commands the statistics, and therefore the dragon has the edge." But don't be fooled, God wins. In fact, he has already won. Blount goes on to says, "The statistics say, 'Death wins. Every single time.' The Resurrection says, 'Hold on. Not so fast. . . .'"[1] As we come to the final cycle of Revelation, we witness the power of Christ as God's enemies—sin, death, and the devil—are destroyed and in newness is ushered into this world.

FAITHFUL AND TRUE

With the destruction of the whore complete, God's wrath is directed toward the beast and false prophet. God sends a final rider on a white horse to be his champion. The rider's name is "Faithful and True."

> Then I saw heaven opened, and behold, a white horse! The one sitting on it is called Faithful and True, and in righteousness he judges and makes war. His eyes are like a flame of fire, and on his head are many diadems, and he has a name written that no one knows but himself. He is clothed in a robe dipped in blood, and the name by which he is called is The Word of God. And the armies of heaven, arrayed in fine linen, white and pure, were following him on white horses. From his mouth comes a sharp sword with which to strike down the nations, and he will rule them with a rod of iron. He will tread the winepress of the fury of the wrath of God the Almighty. On his robe and on his thigh he has a name written, King of kings and Lord of lords. (Rev 19:11–16)

1. Blount, *Invasion of the Dead*, 40–41.

There is a lot going on in this brief passage. Jesus' appearance is similar to the vision given in Revelation 1—eyes blazing with flames of fire, dressed in a bloody robe, and a sword coming from his mouth. Jesus comes without the weapons of the world or the might of worldly power. Instead, the weapon in his mouth, a sword which is the Word of God, is the only thing he has to do battle with God's foes (Rev 1:16; 2:12; 19:15). The army of heaven wears fine linen like the bride (Rev 19:8). Christ treads the winepress of God's wrath which was first mentioned in Revelation 14:20. And his many crowns signify that he is the true "King of kings and Lord of lords."

In the midst of such imagery it is easy to miss one of the most important points, namely, Jesus' robe is "dipped in blood" (Rev 19:13). Normally, when there is a battle the victor is victorious because the enemy's blood has been shed. But Christ rides into battle with his own blood on him. This is what the saints did earlier in Revelation as they washed their robes in the blood of the Lamb (Rev 7:14). They know there is power in the blood.

In 1861, as the Civil War was in its infancy, the abolitionist and poet Julia Ward Howe reviewed "Company K" of the Sixth Wisconsin Volunteer Infantry outside of Washington on Upton Hill. As she was watched the company march, she heard the soldiers sing "John Brown's Body," which praised the abolitionist who had been hanged for his raid on Harper's Ferry. That evening she awoke from sleep with new lyrics for the tune in her head. The text was inspired by Revelation 19:

> *Mine eyes have seen the glory of the coming of the Lord:*
> *He is trampling out the vintage where the grapes of wrath are stored;*
> *He hath loosed the fateful lightning of His terrible swift sword:*
> *His truth is marching on.*
> *Glory, glory, hallelujah! Glory, glory, hallelujah!*
> *Glory, glory, hallelujah! His truth is marching on.*[2]

2. Howe, "Battle Hymn of the Republic," *Lutheran Book of Worship*, Minneapolis: Augsburg (1979), 332, verse 1 with refrain.

Julia Ward Howe understood that strength does not come from effort, political affiliation, military weapons, financial status, or the like. Instead, it comes from the Lord whose truth is marching on.

The scene in John's vision advances as an angel calls in birds of prey to devour the flesh of God's enemies. This is a gruesome end to those who drank from the harlot's cup that contained the blood of the saints (Rev 17:6).

> Then I saw an angel standing in the sun, and with a loud voice he called to all the birds that fly directly overhead, "Come, gather for the great supper of God, to eat the flesh of kings, the flesh of captains, the flesh of mighty men, the flesh of horses and their riders, and the flesh of all men, both free and slave, both small and great." (Rev 19:17–18)

The vision advances once again as John sees the great battle, Armageddon, that was first mentioned in Revelation 16:16.[3] One does not have to guess what happens to the beast and false prophet: They oppose God and meet a fate similar to the harlot's end.

> And I saw the beast and the kings of the earth with their armies gathered to make war against him who was sitting on the horse and against his army. And the beast was captured, and with it the false prophet who in its presence had done the signs by which he deceived those who had received the mark of the beast and those who worshiped its image. These two were thrown alive into the lake of fire that burns with sulfur. And the rest were slain by the sword that came from the mouth of him who was sitting on the horse, and all the birds were gorged with their flesh. (Rev 19:19–21)

The beast and the false prophet are cast into the lake of fire, that is, into the eternal condemnation of hell. They have earned their place in the lake of fire because they had earlier attempted to turn the earth into a living hell.

---

3. Schüssler Fiorenza, *Revelation*, 105.

Just as with God's love and justice in a previous cycle, the notion of hell as eternal punishment can come across as morally repugnant and move us to ask how a God who is good can cast people into eternal punishment. Though the sentiment behind the question is good, it does miss the point. In order for God to say, "Yes," God must also be able to say, "No." For instance, God's liberation of the Hebrew slaves meant that Pharaoh and his armies had to be destroyed (Exod 1–15). In order to save, God had to condemn.

These words about the "lake of fire" serve as another warning to God's people. Those who side with the beast will be defeated. Their fate is similar to the ones they serve. However, it is not too late. These words are spoken as mercy for the hearer: Come out of her, my people (Rev 18:4). Renounce the beast and worship the Lamb.

THE BINDING OF SATAN

John's focus shifts to a new character as we see an angel with a key in one hand and a chain in the other. At the end of the chain is the dragon. This is the dragon who tried to usurp Christ's throne (Rev 12:3), tried to destroy Christ at birth (Rev 12:4–5), and then tried to consume the woman and her children in the wilderness (Rev 12:13–17). The dragon is Satan, the ancient foe.

> Then I saw an angel coming down from heaven, holding in his hand the key to the bottomless pit and a great chain. And he seized the dragon, that ancient serpent, who is the devil and Satan, and bound him for a thousand years, and threw him into the pit, and shut it and sealed it over him, so that he might not deceive the nations any longer, until the thousand years were ended. After that he must be released for a little while. (Rev 20:1–3)

The Angel with the Key to the Bottomless Pit
by Albrecht Dürer

Description (Figure 9): Satan is chained and thrown into the pit. He has a prison sentence of a thousand years. In the sky above, the birds are ready to devour the enemies of God.

142

The angel of the Lord binds Satan (see fig. 9), another demonstration that Satan's territory is limited. Satan has not only been cast out of heaven (Rev 12:9), but now is also imprisoned for a millennium (Rev 20:3). Interpreters have struggled to make sense of this thousand-year sentence as it relates to human history. There are three main ways people have interpreted the thousand-year sentence. Here are summaries of the three positions:

Pre-millennialism: Christ returns to begin his literal thousand-year reign (millennium) and binds Satan. The saints who are raptured join the martyrs in heaven for that period while the 144,000 (often thought to be Israel) remain on the earth. At the end of the millennium, Satan is released and is destroyed. At that time, Christ, the martyrs who have been raptured, and the present faithful humans still living will reign in the New Jerusalem that will be established on earth. The worldview of pre-millennialist is that the world is getting worse and only Christ's return will fix it. There is a major focus on evangelism because the goal is to save as many people as possible before the rapture. This position is promoted in the *Left Behind* series.

Post-millennialism: The millennium begins with Jesus, whose life, death, and resurrection usher in the kingdom of God. During this era (not a literal thousand years but a complete era of time) the kingdom of God advances and expands through the preaching of the gospel. It is Christ's victory over the grave along with the ongoing advancement of the gospel that binds Satan over the span of the millennium and brings peace to the world. After the world becomes Christian, the millennium-long reign ends and Christ will return to judge the living and the dead. It is at his return that a rapture will occur, calling up believers to join Jesus in heaven as he descends to the earth. At that time, the New Jerusalem will be established on earth. The worldview of post-millennialists is that Christ has conquered and the world is getting better. The human task is to accomplish the repair of a broken world and bring about an earlier return of Christ. The focus is on the betterment of society. This view was popular among American Protestants during the Progressive Movement of the nineteenth century. It lost prominence as the two World Wars, the Great Depression, the Holocaust and other attempts at genocide, the Cold War, and other challenges of the last century forced people to see how impossible reform and human progress were.

Amillennialism: This view understands the language of Revelation 20 as symbolic language used to proclaim a true reality in the same way that John's gospel tells the story of Christ to reveal a hidden truth about Jesus, sinners, and the world. In other words, the thousand years in this passage points to God's rule that was inaugurated at Christ's resurrection and at which point Satan was cast out of heaven. Christ already reigns at the right hand of the Father in the present and gives his Spirit to the church to proclaim the gospel. Christ is "already and not yet" victorious over Satan (thus Satan is both bound and still roaming the earth). Until Christ's return, a tension exists on earth between the righteous and the wicked. When Christ returns, he will establish the New Jerusalem on earth. The worldview of amellennialists is that Christ is Lord of the world and thus the focus is on evangelism and renewal of society. Major proponents include Saint Augustine, Martin Luther, John Calvin, Orthodox Churches, Roman Catholic, Lutherans, and the Reformed.

Each of these positions has its strengths and weaknesses. For instance, pre-millennialists focus on the Great Commission to make disciples of all nations (Matt 28:18–20) because they want many new believers to join Christians in heaven. Yet too often people with this position fail to engage this world because they think it is all going to burn anyway. Post-millennialists focus on the Great Commandment to love (Matt 22:36–40) because they must renew the earth before Christ comes again. However, after major wars in the past century, one wonders if the world is getting better. Finally, amillennialists care for both evangelism and renewing of society. Whatever approach becomes the lens for this passage, though, it's important to remember that *all* of these positions affirm the return of Christ and the establishment of the New Jerusalem. As we have seen time and again in Revelation, this is a story about God's victory over sin, death, and the devil in the historical events of Christ's death and resurrection.

VINDICATION OF THE SAINTS

With Satan's defeat, we now see the vindication of the saints who had been martyred. These are the saints who cried out for vindication in an earlier cycle (Rev 6:10). These are also the ones who said God's mercy is also God's justice (Rev 16:7).

> Then I saw thrones, and seated on them were those to whom the authority to judge was committed. Also I saw the souls of those who had been beheaded for the testimony of Jesus and for the word of God, and those who had not worshiped the beast or its image and had not received its mark on their foreheads or their hands. They came to life and reigned with Christ for a thousand years. The rest of the dead did not come to life until the thousand years were ended. This is the first resurrection. Blessed and holy is the one who shares in the first resurrection! Over such the second death has no power, but they will be priests of God and of Christ, and they will reign with him for a thousand years. (Rev 20:4–6)

As with the previous passage, how we understand the millennium determines how we understand these verses, and questions can arise. For instance, do the saints reign with God in heaven or on earth? We do not know where they reign, but we do know their new life of faith always happens in proximity to Christ. As Craig Koester notes, "Each time we might expect him to say that they reigned on earth, [John] says they 'reigned with Christ'" (Rev 20:4, 6).[4] Second, we do not know what the "first resurrection" means,

---

4. Koester, *Revelation and the End of All Things*, 185.

but we do know that it highlights the priority of the saints who will reign with Christ as priests (Rev 1:6; 5:10).

Combine this promise with the manner in which these saints died (namely, martyrdom), and we can understand what is being said here. Their deaths as martyrs make it appear as though they were forsaken. However, this could not be further from the case. Like so much in Revelation, behind what we see and experience in the world lies a different and true reality. The gruesome end for the martyred saints is not the last word, for they have proximity to Christ and priority in the resurrection, as it should be.

Stephen was the first Christian martyr. In the book of Acts 6–7 we read about his death by stoning at the hands of Jerusalem's religious leaders. Stephen could have renounced Christ, but he stayed faithful in his witness. Stephen could have cursed his killers but prayed for them instead. As Stephen died, he saw Christ sitting at the right hand of God welcoming him home. This story is reflected in the hymn "The Son of God Goes Forth to War":

The Son of God goes forth to war
A kingly crown to gain.
His blood-red banner streams afar;
Who follows in His train?
Who best can drink His cup of woe,
Triumphant over pain,
Who patient bears his cross below—
He follows in His train.

The martyr first, whose eagle eye
Could pierce beyond the grave,
Who saw his Master in the sky
And called on Him to save.
Like Him, with pardon on His tongue,
In midst of mortal pain,
He prayed for them that did the wrong—
Who follows in his train?[5]

---

5. Reginald Heber, "The Son of God Goes Forth to War," *Lutheran Book of Worship* (Minneapolis: Augsburg, 1979), 183, verses 1 and 2.

SATAN IS DESTROYED

When the thousand-year sentence ends, Satan is released from his prison. An obvious question is whether the jail time rehabilitated the dragon. We are given the answer in the following verses:

> And when the thousand years are ended, Satan will be released from his prison and will come out to deceive the nations that are at the four corners of the earth, Gog and Magog, to gather them for battle; their number is like the sand of the sea. And they marched up over the broad plain of the earth and surrounded the camp of the saints and the beloved city, but fire came down from heaven and consumed them, and the devil who had deceived them was thrown into the lake of fire and sulfur where the beast and the false prophet were, and they will be tormented day and night forever and ever. (Rev 20:7–10)

Satan is not rehabilitated. After being cast out of heaven, he turns to attack the earth. After having been cast into jail and released, he now gathers Gog and Magog for an attack. This is an allusion to a prophecy mentioned in Ezekiel 38–39 where the "Son of man" will attack Israel's enemy "Gog" in the land of Magog.[6] It is clear that Satan will not cease his attack on those who stand with God until the Evil One ceases to exist. That is exactly what happens. The devil is cast into the lake of fire joining the beast and false prophet (Rev 19:20). With the devil, the beast, and false prophet destroyed, God must destroy the final enemy, namely, death.

> Then I saw a great white throne and him who was seated on it. From his presence earth and sky fled away, and no place was found for them. And I saw the dead, great and small, standing before the throne, and books were opened. Then another book was opened, which is the book of life. And the dead were judged by what was written in the books, according to what they had done. And the sea gave up the dead who were in it, Death and

6. Caird, *Revelation of St. John*, 256.

> Hades gave up the dead who were in them, and they were judged, each one of them, according to what they had done. Then Death and Hades were thrown into the lake of fire. This is the second death, the lake of fire. And if anyone's name was not found written in the book of life, he was thrown into the lake of fire. (Rev 20:11–15)

On this Judgment Day, God sits on the white throne. Open before God are two sets of books. The first book is the book of life. The other set of books includes those in which the dead are judged. There are two different books because one set reminds us that our actions matter while the other tells us that God's grace is enough. As Craig Koester explains, "The book of life is like a civic record, in which the citizens of the city of God have their names inscribed from the foundation of the world (Rev 13:8; 17:8), which means that they cannot obtain access to the book of life by their own efforts, but are included in the book as an act of divine grace." The other set of books records what people did during their lives. Koester continues, "On the day of judgment, these books will be opened and people will be held accountable for their actions."[7]

In *The Lion, the Witch, and the Wardrobe,* C. S. Lewis does a marvelous job of holding judgment and mercy together when Edmund meets the great lion Aslan, who is the Christ figure. Edmund, a boy from the real world, is regarded in the land of Narnia as a "son of Adam." One could say his name was written in the book of life. However, while he is held in high esteem and is granted great privilege, Edmund also had betrayed his family, and his actions have consequences. Edmund must face Aslan. The deeds of his life lay exposed before Aslan. The judgment is serious because sin is serious. However, he is a "son of Adam" and Aslan has grace toward him. In fact, Lewis describes the conversation with these words: "There is no need to tell you (and no one ever heard) what Aslan was saying but it was a conversation which Edmund never forgot."[8] Judgment Day is like that. We stand before God with our

---

7. Koester, *Revelation and the End of All Things,* 189–90.
8. Lewis, *The Lion, the Witch and the Wardrobe,* 135.

lives exposed. There is much that Christ will say to us. Our deeds matter. However, because of Jesus' death, our sins are forgiven and our names are written in the book of life.

Judgment Day ends with Death itself being thrown into the lake of fire. This is called the "second death" because it is the final death. Now, God's work of judging the nations is over. Now the words of Revelation 11:18 have come to pass: "The nations raged, but your wrath came, and the time for the dead to be judged, and for rewarding your servants, the prophets and saints, and those who fear your name, both small and great, and for destroying the destroyers of the earth." All of God's enemies have been destroyed. God is faithful and true to his promises.

In the face of her death, Vicki reminded me that the rider's name is "Faithful and True." It's what she clung to and what she wanted me to lay hold of as well. Christ, who has the keys to death and hades (Rev 1:18), strengthened her in her weakness. While it may look like the dragon has the upper hand in this world, the resurrection changes everything. There is power in his blood!

Refocus Questions

1. Why is it important that Christ's name is "Faithful and True?"

2. Christ's only weapon in battling evil is the sword (which is the Word of God). How does he use that weapon? Is it a sword that we can wield?

3. Which view of the millennium, if any, were you taught? Of these three views, which one do you think makes the most sense now?

4. Why does it matter how a person sees the end of the world?

5. This cycle of Revelation tells us the beast, the false prophet, Satan, and death are all destroyed in the lake of fire. Which of these are you happiest about being destroyed? Why?

6. What is one of your deeds that will be written in the book of deeds?

7. Is your name written in the book of life? How might you know? (See John 3:16–17.)

REVELATION 21–22

Is God Making You New?

And he who was seated on the throne said, "Behold, I am making all things new." Also he said, "Write this down, for these words are trustworthy and true." (Rev 18:4–5)

WHEN MY DAUGHTER ABIGAIL was five, she proved herself to be an astute theologian. She asked me if there would be elephants in heaven. I asked her what she thought, and her response amazed me. She said, "Of course elephants will be in heaven, because when you get dirty from playing you will need a shower, and there is no better shower than having an elephant spray you with water." I think Abby was on to something.

The Bible speaks of animals in heaven. The prophet Isaiah says the New Jerusalem will be a place where *"the wolf shall dwell with the lamb, and the leopard shall lie down with the young goat, and the calf and the lion and the fattened calf together; and a little child shall lead them. The cow and the bear shall graze; their young shall lie down together; and the lion shall eat straw like the ox. The nursing child shall play over the hole of the cobra, and the weaned child shall put his hand on the adder's den"* (Isa 11:6–8). Of course this is not an exhaustive list. But it does assert that, in the glorious future, the Lord will eliminate conflicts among animals and between animals and humans. Former predators will live peacefully with their former prey. Little children will have nothing to fear from carnivorous beasts or venomous snakes. There will be animals in heaven.

What I appreciate about Abigail's comment was her thought of the New Jerusalem as a real place to play, to get dirty, and to take showers. This is a far cry from popular sentiment that speaks of heaven as a spiritual realm where human souls have abandoned the burden of their bodies and they float around playing harps on puffy clouds. Talk about boring! God has a much greater future for us than mindless clouds. In the final chapters of Revelation we are given a picture of the New Jerusalem with its cosmic, social, political, and sacred dimensions.

THE FINAL VISION

Readers of Revelation have seen many visions while reading this book: the heavenly throne room, the twenty-four elders, the four horsemen, the dragon, the beast and false prophet, the whore, and the lake of fire, to name a few. There have also been visions of Christ who holds the keys of death and hades, of Jesus who is the worthy lamb who opens the scroll, and the rider whose name is "Faithful and True." Apocalypse means to "uncover," and Revelation does just that as it pulls back the curtain on Christ's victory over God's foes. For its final vision, Revelation paints one last picture with its description of the New Jerusalem.

> Then I saw a new heaven and a new earth, for the first heaven and the first earth had passed away, and the sea was no more. And I saw the holy city, new Jerusalem, coming down out of heaven from God, prepared as a bride adorned for her husband. And I heard a loud voice from the throne saying, "Behold, the dwelling place of God is with man. He will dwell with them, and they will be his people, and God himself will be with them as their

God. He will wipe away every tear from their eyes, and
death shall be no more, neither shall there be mourning, nor crying, nor pain anymore, for the former things
have passed away." And he who was seated on the throne
said, "Behold, I am making all things new." Also he said,
"Write this down, for these words are trustworthy and
true." And he said to me, "It is done! I am the Alpha and
the Omega, the beginning and the end. To the thirsty I
will give from the spring of the water of life without pay-
ment. The one who conquers will have this heritage, and
I will be his God and he will be my son. But as for the
cowardly, the faithless, the detestable, as for murderers,
the sexually immoral, sorcerers, idolaters, and all liars,
their portion will be in the lake that burns with fire and
sulfur, which is the second death." (Rev 21:1–8)

John is told by the angel to look, and he sees the New Jerusalem *coming down* from heaven. The direction is significant because
too often we think heaven is a place to which we journey. A common vision of heaven is that our souls are released from our bodies
and they float up to the Great Beyond. But in John's vision heaven
is something that comes to us. Christians do not need to escape
this world, because God's desire is to restore this world rather than
destroy it.

Of course, the restoration is something only God can complete. We see God's work as he makes the creation new. Because
God has destroyed death, he is free to wipe away our tears. When
the battle to save us from sin, death, and the devil is won, we can
see things differently. Our pain in this life now belongs to the former things. They, along with the enemies of God are removed from
us. My friend Ken Sundet Jones taught me that in the German
language the term for "Judgment Day" is translated "the Youngest
Day." This makes sense because everything connected with the old
life under the power of evil is now made new.

After not just winning the battle but also taking the entire
battlefield as his own territory, God signals that the whole bloody

mess is about to be cleaned up when he says, "It is done!" In Greek, these are the same words Christ spoke from the cross when he said, "It is finished" (John 19:30). Just as Christ's defeat of death was finished on the cross and new life came with the empty tomb, God the creator has conquered all his enemies and now remakes creation. The wilderness that earlier came to the aid of God's people (Rev 12) has been restored.

The vision continues as one of the angels who had poured one of the seven bowls of wrath now speaks of a much happier day.

> Then came one of the seven angels who had the seven bowls full of the seven last plagues and spoke to me, saying, "Come, I will show you the Bride, the wife of the Lamb." And he carried me away in the Spirit to a great, high mountain, and showed me the holy city Jerusalem coming down out of heaven from God, having the glory of God, its radiance like a most rare jewel, like a jasper, clear as crystal. It had a great, high wall, with twelve gates, and at the gates twelve angels, and on the gates the names of the twelve tribes of the sons of Israel were inscribed—on the east three gates, on the north three gates, on the south three gates, and on the west three gates. And the wall of the city had twelve foundations, and on them were the twelve names of the twelve apostles of the Lamb. (Rev 21:9–14)

This is the wedding mention in Revelation 19. The New Jerusalem is viewed socially as the bride who is betrothed to the Lamb. The New Jerusalem is adorned with beauty, and the twelve gates have the names of the twelve tribes of Israel. In the Old Testament, God made a covenant with Abraham and his descendants (Gen 12:1–3), and now we see that God has been faithful to his promise. The relationship is whole. The covenant was like an engagement ring until the wedding. Now it is time to consummate the marriage. Now is the time when God dwells with us.

John's description of the New Jerusalem's architecture is rich with details. They speak of the political reality of the New Jerusalem.

> And the one who spoke with me had a measuring rod of gold to measure the city and its gates and walls. The city lies foursquare, its length the same as its width. And he measured the city with his rod, 12,000 stadia. Its length and width and height are equal. He also measured its wall, 144 cubits by human measurement, which is also an angel's measurement. The wall was built of jasper, while the city was pure gold, like clear glass. The foundations of the wall of the city were adorned with every kind of jewel. The first was jasper, the second sapphire, the third agate, the fourth emerald, the fifth onyx, the sixth carnelian, the seventh chrysolite, the eighth beryl, the ninth topaz, the tenth chrysoprase, the eleventh jacinth, the twelfth amethyst. And the twelve gates were twelve pearls, each of the gates made of a single pearl, and the street of the city was pure gold, like transparent glass. (Rev 21:15–21)

It is not surprising that architecture has political ramifications. Buildings are often created to make statements. Skyscrapers and high-rises paint a city's skyline, proclaiming its greatness. Sport arenas are constructed to advertise a team and a company. Rome built significant structures like the Colosseum to illustrate its power. Washington, DC, has monuments to great leaders in this country.

The city of God is no different. Taken literally, the sheer size is impressive as it covers 1400 miles squared (about half the size of the continental United States). The walls are 200 feet thick and are decorated with precious stones. Powerful Rome had streets made out of bricks and buildings made of marble, but in the New Jerusalem the streets and buildings are made of gold. The size and grandeur of the New Jerusalem is significant. Craig Koester explains, "Ezekiel had a vision of a restored Jerusalem that measured only 1.5 square miles. John speaks of a New Jerusalem that will be a thousand times greater than this, affirming that God will both keep and surpass the promises that were made through the prophets."[9]

The fact that the New Jerusalem is shaped as a cube suggests that the holy city is a sanctuary and next we learn about the city's sacred dimensions.

> And I saw no temple in the city, for its temple is the Lord God the Almighty and the Lamb. And the city has no need of sun or moon to shine on it, for the glory of God gives it light, and its lamp is the Lamb. By its light will the nations walk, and the kings of the earth will bring their glory into it, and its gates will never be shut by day—and there will be no night there. They will bring into it the glory and the honor of the nations. But nothing unclean will ever enter it, nor anyone who does what is detestable or false, but only those who are written in the Lamb's book of life. (Rev 21:22–27)

There is no temple in the city. There is no need for a temple, because God is there. There is no need for sun or moon, because God and the Lamb illumine the city. Even the earth's rulers enter to pay homage to God. The arrival of the nations, along with the sovereigns who represent individual cultures, signify the expansive vision of worship.[10] We can say the multitudes have truly arrived when all these people from every nation, tribe, peoples, and language are gathered (Rev 7:9).

Because the New Jerusalem's gates never close, all are welcome to walk in and enjoy what it has to offer. Heaven is not a place to lock people out, but rather a place to let people enter. The nations can enter because the New Jerusalem is a place for the healing of the nations. This is explained in the following verses:

> Then the angel showed me the river of the water of life, bright as crystal, flowing from the throne of God and of the Lamb through the middle of the street of the city; also, on either side of the river, the tree of life with its

---

9. Koester, *Revelation and the End of All Things*, 196.

10. Mouw, *When the Kings Come Marching In*, 50.

twelve kinds of fruit, yielding its fruit each month. The leaves of the tree were for the healing of the nations. No longer will there be anything accursed, but the throne of God and of the Lamb will be in it, and his servants will worship him. They will see his face, and his name will be on their foreheads. And night will be no more. They will need no light of lamp or sun, for the Lord God will be their light, and they will reign forever and ever. (Rev 22:1–5)

In the city is the tree of life. After humanity fell by eating the forbidden fruit, humanity has been separated from the tree of life (Gen 3:1–24). In the New Jerusalem, the tree is there. The leaves that from the tree fall into the river of life bring healing to the nations.

In the summer of 1864 at the height of the Civil War, Robert Lowry was the pastor of a congregation in Brooklyn, New York. On a sweltering day in July, with the war in full force, Lowry began thinking about the last chapter of Revelation. In the face of exhaustion at the slow progress of the war and the immense loss of life, he longed for the river of life that would not only cool him down, but also bring the healing of the nations. Inspired by John's vision, he wrote the words that became the hymn "Shall We Gather at the River."

> *Shall we gather at the river,*
> *Where bright angel feet have trod,*
> *With its crystal tide forever*
> *Flowing by the throne of God?*
>
> *Yes, we'll gather at the river,*
> *The beautiful, the beautiful river;*
> *Gather with the saints at the river*
> *That flows by the throne of God.*[11]

With the nations healed from the tree of life, the people can now see God face to face. The last time this happened was

---

11. Lowry, "Shall We Gather at the River," verse 1 with refrain.

in Genesis 2, prior to humanity's fall and the entrance of sin and death. Now everything has been healed. Our relationship with each other and with God are mended. With such healing, the angel finishes the vision with the following words:

> And he said to me, "These words are trustworthy and true. And the Lord, the God of the spirits of the prophets, has sent his angel to show his servants what must soon take place." "And behold, I am coming soon. Blessed is the one who keeps the words of the prophecy of this book." (Rev 22:6–7)

The vision has promised that heaven is much more than mindless clouds. It has cosmic, social, political, and sacred dimensions to it. It is a place of healing. We can trust what these words promise, because God is trustworthy and true.

AMEN, COME LORD JESUS!

So how are we to live as we wait that glorious day? In his postscript, John reminds us of themes that appear throughout the book. These themes are meant to orient our lives as we wait and turn us in faith toward God in the meantime. John writes:

> I, John, am the one who heard and saw these things. And when I heard and saw them, I fell down to worship at the feet of the angel who showed them to me, but he said to me, "You must not do that! I am a fellow servant with you and your brothers the prophets, and with those who keep the words of this book. Worship God." (Rev 22:8–9)

Three things in Revelation have great consequence. John's vision tells us that some things matter most.

Worship matters. Earlier in John's vision God is worshiped as the creator, and Jesus is worshiped for opening the scroll (Rev 4–5). The beast sought worship for himself and tried to lure the nations to worship him through the false prophet (Rev 13). Twice John was so overwhelmed by his vision that he tried to worship the angel. Both times he was told to worship God (Rev 19:10; 22:9). Humanity was made to worship God and the Lamb.

> And he said to me, "Do not seal up the words of the prophecy of this book, for the time is near. Let the evil-doer still do evil, and the filthy still be filthy, and the righteous still do right, and the holy still be holy." (Rev 22:10–11)

Evangelism matters. The picture of what God does in John's vision is not meant to be kept to oneself. The world needs witnesses to proclaim the faith. When the two witnesses proclaimed the gospel, the city was saved (Rev 11). Christians are called to do the same. Only the word of God creates faith (Rom 10:17).

> "Behold, I am coming soon, bringing my recompense with me, to repay each one for what he has done. I am the Alpha and the Omega, the first and the last, the be-ginning and the end." Blessed are those who wash their robes, so that they may have the right to the tree of life and that they may enter the city by the gates. Outside are the dogs and sorcerers and the sexually immoral and murderers and idolaters, and everyone who loves and practices falsehood. (Rev 22:12–15)

What we believe matters. When those who trust God wash their robes in the blood of the Lamb, they show their trust in Christ's saving work for them on the cross and receive access to the city of God. Those who trust themselves drink from the cup of the whore (Rev 18:3). The book of deeds in Revelation reveals the deeds of the unfaithful (Rev 20:11–15).

As John is finishing up his postscript, Jesus interrupts with one final word to the churches. This word is filled with invitation:

> "I, Jesus, have sent my angel to testify to you about these things for the churches. I am the root and the descen-dant of David, the bright morning star." The Spirit and the Bride say, "Come." And let the one who hears say, "Come." And let the one who is thirsty come; let the one

who desires take the water of life without price. I warn
everyone who hears the words of the prophecy of this
book: if anyone adds to them, God will add to him the
plagues described in this book, and if anyone takes away
from the words of the book of this prophecy, God will
take away his share in the tree of life and in the holy
city, which are described in this book. He who testifies
to these things says, "Surely I am coming soon." (Rev
22:18–19)

The gates to the city of God never close. The invitation is for
all. Jesus stands at the door and knocks (Rev 3:20). The invitation
is also for those who have been consumed by the whore. Come out
of her my people (Rev 18:4). The invitation is for those who are
broken and those in need of forgiveness. With God there is always
forgiveness. With God there is healing water to drink. We do not
have to pay for it. Christ paid with his blood. The New Jerusalem
is for all of us.

There is nothing more to say. God's Word is enough. There
is no need to take away from it or add to it. Consume it like John
consumed the scroll (Rev 10:8–11). Yes, it can be bitter in its challenge, but it will also be as sweet as honey. It is the only weapon
Christ needed to battle evil (Rev 1:16; 19:15). It is the only weapon
we need.

The Revelation is complete. Christ is coming soon. Whenever
the truth is proclaimed, Christ is near. John ends with these words:

Amen. Come, Lord Jesus! The grace of the Lord Jesus be
with all. Amen. (Rev 22:20–21)

We are not given all the details on what the New Jerusalem
will be like. There might be flights on saddled pterodactyls, swim-
ming pools filled with both toddlers and great white sharks, and
even Abby's hoped-for showers from elephants. Everything that
God gives is good. We do not know all the details. However, we
know that God makes all things new. That means us! One can say
"Amen. Yup. That's right. God is mine, and I am his." With its final
verse, Revelation bids us to call out in hope and faith for Christ to

come: "Christ, come into our hearts. Christ, come into our homes. Christ, come into our churches. Christ, you hold the keys to death and hades. Come and resurrect. Come, destroy our enemies and lead us to everlasting life. Come and make us new." Until he returns, the grace of the Lord Jesus be with us all!

Refocus Questions

1. What is one thing you want to do in the New Jerusalem?

2. Who is one person you want to see?

3. Why is it important that those present in the New Jerusalem aren't limited to a specific nation, group, or class?

4. How significant is it that the gates never close?

5. Since we no longer have a temple, will we "have church" in heaven?

6. The tree of life brings the healing of the nations. What are a few things in this world that you would like to see healed? What are ways God is using you to bring healing to the nations?

7. How do the words: "Amen, Come Lord Jesus," affect you now that you have read the book of Revelation?

Afterword

THE BOOK OF REVELATION is not only filled with singing, but its words have inspired many hymns and songs such as "Holy, Holy, Holy;" "Shall We Gather at the River;" "Crown Him with Many Crowns;" and "The Battle Hymn of the Republic," to name a few. Just as the book of Revelation demands participation, so does the singing of music. The question being asked today is whether our young adults will join in the song of faith.

In my work with college students over the last 12 years I have seen huge shifts in musical taste, fashion sense, cultural references and general attitudes about life, work and faith. Although I was closer in age and cultural familiarity when I began my work in my early twenties, it was only a few years before I realized I had almost nothing in common with the students I was trying to reach. Bothersome questions began to creep in: "what do I have in common with these people? What can I possibly offer them?"

Such a question exposed my immaturity and lack of faith, and mercifully drove me back to the only true source of hope: Jesus Christ. I can wear myself out trying to keep up with student culture, humor and music, but in the end the best thing I can give them is Jesus himself. This Jesus—-who was the only hope of the Irish missionaries, the Reformers and the Oxford Movement—-is still the hope of the young in the 21st century. He is ahead of us in every way, and is powerfully at work in the upcoming generations. The moment we cease to believe that is the moment we've stepped out of God's power and into our own strength.

As a worship leader, I am seeing young people encounter God and have their lives changed. I am seeing young people who are willing to serve, to learn, to share the gospel and to worship with a vibrancy and intensity that makes my jaw drop. What's more, they are hungry. Hungry to be shaped, to be trained, and to be disciplined (yes, disciplined!) by their elders in the faith. They are singing and living the very faith Revelation proclaims.

There's something wonderful about the fact that the good news is good news for every age, every culture and every nation. The history of the Church has many ups and downs, victories and embarrassments—but the central destination, the place where we are all headed—is utterly and immutably secure. Jesus has been on the throne, is now on the throne, and will be on the throne. May we be the kinds of leaders who empower young people to carry the faith to the next generation, so that a generation yet unborn would know that Jesus Christ, the Lamb of God, is *worthy to receive power and wealth and wisdom and might and honor and glory and blessing* (Rev 5:12)!

Joel Patterson
Westmont College, Santa Barbara
2016

Bibliography

Augustine. *Confessions*. London: Penguin Classics, 1961.

Bar-Zohar, Michael. *Beyond Hitler's Grasp: The Historic Rescue of Bulgaria's Jews*. Avon: Adam's Media, 1998.

Bassi, Lauri. *Good Company: Business Success in the Worthiness Era*. San Francisco: Berrett, 2011.

Bauckham, Richard. *The Climax of Prophecy: Studies on the Book of Revelation*. Edinburgh: T. & T. Clark: London, 2005.

———. *The Theology of the Book of Revelation*. Cambridge: Cambridge University Press, 1993.

Bendle, Mervyn F. "Apocalyptic Imagination and Popular Culture." *Journal of Religion and Popular Culture* 11 (2005) 1. http://www.utpjournals.press/doi/abs/10.3138/jrpc.11.1.001?journalCode=jrpc.

Blount, Brian. *Invasion of the Dead: Preaching Resurrection*. Louisville: Westminster, 2014.

Boring, M. Eugene. *Revelation*. Interpretation. Louisville: John Knox, 1989.

Brighton, Louis. *Revelation*. Concordia. St. Louis: Concordia, 1999.

Caird, G. B. *The Revelation of Saint John*. Peabody: Hendrickson, 1966.

Capon, Robert Farrar. *The Parables of the Kingdom*. Grand Rapids: Zondervan, 1985.

Chan, Fran. "Rethinking Outreach." Exponential West Conference, October 7, 2014, Los Angeles.

Collins, Adela Yarbro. *Crisis and Catharsis: The Power of Apocalypse*. Philadelphia: Westminster, 1984.

Elliot, Elisabeth. *Through Gates of Splendor*. Wheaton: Tyndale, 1981.

Evangelical Lutheran Worship. Hymnal. Minneapolis: Augsburg Fortress, 2006.

Gilbreath, Edward. *Birmingham Revolution: Martin Luther King Jr.'s Epic Challenge to the Church*. Downers Grove: InterVarsity, 2013.

Gonzales, Justo L. *The Story of Christianity: The Early Church to the Dawn of the Reformation*. New York: HarperCollins, 2010.

Hampton, Keith, et al. "Social Media and the 'Spiral of Silence.'" *Pew Research Center*. August 26, 2014. http://www.pewinternet.org/2014/08/26/social-media-and-the-spiral-of-silence.

Haught, John F. "Christianity and Ecology." In *The Sacred Earth: Religion, Nature, Environment*, edited by Roger S. Gottlieb, 232–47. New York: Routledge, 2002.

Hemer, Colin J. *The Letters to the Seven Churches of Asia in Their Local Setting*. Grand Rapids: Eerdmans, 2001.

Hengel, Martin. *Crucifixion in the Ancient World and the Folly of the Message of the Cross*. Minneapolis: Fortress, 1977.

Heschel, Abraham. *The Prophets: An Introduction*. New York: Harper, 1962.

Hillenbrand, Laura. *Unbroken: A World War II Story of Survival, Resilience, and Redemption*. New York: Random House, 2010.

Hochschild, Adam. *Bury the Chains: Prophets and Rebels in the Fight to Free an Empire's Slaves*. New York: Houghton, 2005.

Kinnaman, David. *You Lost Me: Why Young Christians Are Leaving Church and Rethinking Christianity*. Grand Rapids: Baker, 2011.

Koester, Craig. *Revelation: A New Translation with Introduction and Commentary*. Anchor Bible. New Haven: Yale, 2014.

———. *Revelation and the End of All Things*. Grand Rapids: Eerdmans, 2001.

Lewis, C. S. *God in the Dock: Essays on Theology and Ethics*. Edited by Walter Hooper. Grand Rapids: Eerdmans, 1970.

———. *The Lion, the Witch, and the Wardrobe*. New York: Scholastic, 1995.

Lindsey, Hal. *The Late Great Planet Earth*. Grand Rapids: Zondervan, 1970.

Luther, Martin. *Career of the Reformer*. Vol. 4. Edited by Helmut T. Lehmann and Lewis W. Spitz. Luther's Works 34. St. Louis: Concordia, 1960.

———. *Lectures on Romans*. Edited by Hilton C. Oswald. Luther's Works 25. St. Louis: Concordia, 1960.

McClennen, Sophia. *America according to Colbert: Satire as Public Pedagogy (Education, Politics, and Public Life)*. New York: Palgrave Macmillan, 2011.

Mouw, Richard J. *When the Kings Come Marching In: Isaiah and the New Jerusalem*. Grand Rapids: Eerdmans, 2002.

Packer, J. I. *Knowing God*. Downers Grove: InterVarsity, 1993.

Peterson, Eugene. "Eat This Book: The Holy Community at Table with the Holy Scripture." *Theology Today* 56 (1999) 5–17. http://www.cslewisinstitute.org/webfm_send/446.

———. *Reversed Thunder: The Revelation of John and the Praying Imagination*. New York: HarperCollins, 1988.

Reich, Robert. *Saving Capitalism: For the Many, Not the Few*. New York: Vintage, 2016.

San Martín, Inés. "On Good Friday, Christians Ponder Modern-Day Martyrdom." *Crux*, April 3, 2015. https://cruxnow.com/faith/2015/04/03/on-good-friday-christians-ponder-modern-day-martyrdom.

Schüssler Fiorenza, Elizabeth. *Revelation: A Vision of a Just World*. Minneapolis: Fortress, 1991.

Stott, John. *Your Mind Matters: The Place of the Mind in the Christian Life*. Downers Grove: InterVarsity, 2006.

Wilkinson, Will. "Satire and Terrorism: Drawing Blood." *Economist*, January 7, 2015. http://www.economist.com/blogs/democracyinamerica/2015/01/satire-and-terrorism.

Wilson, Sarah Hinlicky. "Peace, Peace, When There Is No Peace." *Lutheran Forum* 42 (2008) 3–6.